■ Savory Bread Pudding

Both eggs and cheese are great with basil. Here we add roasted red pepper to contrast with their richness. The pudding makes a savory, filling main course when served with a vegetable or fruit salad; it also makes a good brunch entrée. Use French bread or country-style wheat, a bread with substantial character.

SERVES 6

5 tablespoons (75 ml) unsalted butter

8 slices bread, sliced about 5/8 inch (15 mm) thick

1 small onion, diced; about 3/4 cup (180 ml)

1 small red bell pepper, roasted, peeled, seeded, and diced into 3/4-inch (2-cm) pieces

3 cups (710 ml) milk

2 large cloves garlic, minced

6 extra-large eggs

1 teaspoon (5 ml) salt

Freshly ground pepper

1 cup (240 ml) packed, chopped basil leaves

$1^1/_2$ cups (360 ml) grated sharp cheddar cheese

Preheat oven to 375°F (190°C). Butter a 2-quart (2-l) oval gratin or casserole dish. Butter the bread, using 2 tablespoons (30 ml) of the butter. Cut the bread into cubes, just under an inch (2.5 cm) in size. Set aside.

Melt the remaining 3 tablespoons (45 ml) of the butter in a sauté pan, add the onion and sauté over medium-low heat for 5 minutes, stirring occasionally. Add the bell pepper, stir, and remove from heat.

In a nonreactive saucepan, heat the milk to scalding. Remove from heat and stir in the garlic. Beat the eggs in a bowl with the salt and generously season with pepper. Add about 1/2 cup (120 ml) of the hot milk to the eggs and whisk well. Add the onions and peppers to the eggs, stir, and pour the egg and vegetable mixture into the remaining milk; stir well. Add the basil and stir to combine.

Place half the bread in the prepared baking dish and cover evenly with half the cheese. Pour half the egg and vegetable mixture over the bread and cheese. Repeat with the remaining bread, and then the egg and vegetables; arrange the bread and vegetables with a fork if necessary. Cover the casserole with the remaining cheese.

Have ready enough boiling water to come 1 to $1^1/_2$ inches (2.5 to 4 cm) up the sides of a pan large enough to hold the 2-quart (2-l) baking dish. Carefully place the pan with boiling water in the oven and place the baking dish in the pan. Bake in a hot oven for 30 minutes, until golden brown. Remove the baking dish from the oven and the pan of hot water. Let stand for 5 minutes and serve hot.

■ Thai-Style Noodles with Peanut Basil Sauce

Of course, 'Thai' basil leaves should be used here. However, since 'Thai' basil has a pronounced spicy perfume and a strong anise taste, you could also use a combination of sweet green basil, 'Anise' or 'Licorice' basil, and 'Spice' or 'Cinnamon' basil. I've also used light coconut milk rather than the full-fatted one; both work well. If you don't have coconut milk on hand, try substituting pineapple juice. The flavor is not so authentic and it is a bit more tart, so add a little more sugar or a little less lime juice. During the winter when fresh basil is not readily available I've made this dish using about 2 tablespoons (30 ml) of crumbled, dried basil leaves; it doesn't have the pronounced perfume of the fresh, but the results are tasty.

This dish can be served as an appetizer, a side dish to grilled chicken or fish, or as a main course. To serve as a main course, surround the noodles with fresh steamed broccoli and pass the cold beer.

SERVES 4 AS A MAIN COURSE AND 6 AS AN APPETIZER OR SIDE DISH

About 4 ounces (115 g) snowpeas, topped and tailed
4 ounces (115 g) fresh mung bean sprouts
Salt
8 to 10 ounces (225 to 280 g) dried flat Asian noodles or 14 to 16 ounces
 (400 to 450 g) fresh noodles
1/2 cup (120 ml) crunchy peanut butter
1/2 cup (120 ml) coconut milk
1/2 cup (120 ml) water or stock
About 2 tablespoons (30 ml) lime juice
3 tablespoons (45 ml) tamari soy sauce
1 large clove garlic, finely minced
2 to 3 teaspoons (10 to 15 ml) sugar
3/4 teaspoon (4 ml) ground coriander seed
1 teaspoon (5 ml) hot red pepper flakes, finely ground
About 1 cup (240 ml) 'Thai' basil leaves, cut into shreds
Generous 1/4 cup (60 ml) chopped, dry-roasted peanuts

In a large nonreactive pot, bring water to boil for cooking the noodles. Cut the snowpeas on the diagonal, in half lengthwise. Rinse the sprouts with cold water and drain. When the pasta water boils, add salt and blanch the snowpeas for 45 seconds. Remove the snowpeas with a slotted spoon, drain, and refresh under cold water; drain and set aside.

In a heavy-bottomed, nonreactive saucepan, combine the peanut butter, coconut milk, stock, lime juice, soy sauce, garlic, sugar, coriander, and red pepper. Heat over medium-low heat, stirring occasionally with a whisk, until smooth.

BASIL

An Herb Lover's Guide

BASIL

An Herb Lover's Guide

Thomas DeBaggio
& Susan Belsinger

INTERWEAVE PRESS

Basil
An Herb Lover's Guide
by Thomas DeBaggio and Susan Belsinger

Photography, Joe Coca
Design, Susan Wasinger, Signorella Graphic Arts
Production, Marc McCoy Owens

Text © 1996, Thomas DeBaggio and Susan Belsinger
Photography © 1996, Joe Coca and Interweave Press, Inc.

 Interweave Press
201 East Fourth Street
Loveland, Colorado 80537
USA

Printed in Hong Kong by Sing Cheong

Library of Congress Cataloging-in Publication Data:

DeBaggio, Thomas, 1942–
    Basil : an herb lover's guide / Thomas DeBaggio & Susan Belsinger.
      p.   cm.
    Includes bibliographical references and index.
    ISBN 1-883010-19-5
    1. Cookery, Basil. 2. Basil. I. Belsinger, Susan. II. Title.
TX819.B37D43   1996
641.6'57—dc20   96-27758
                                             CIP

First Printing: IWP—20M:596:CC

To Carolyn Dille, who knows the secrets

and the sensory magic

of the kitchen, and who eagerly accepts the emotional

mysteries of basil and poetry.

■

When have we heard
the noises of the earth the farmers hear,
or seen the signs they see?
VIRGIL, *Georgica I* (trans., David R. Slavitt)

Acknowledgements

We owe a serious debt of gratitude to Arthur O. Tucker of Delaware State University and James E. Simon of Purdue University, two scientists whose research has done much to clarify and advance our knowledge about basil. At our suggestion, they conducted significant research on basil that clarified the botanical nomenclature and essential oil content of this herb. In Delaware, Dr. Tucker carefully examined many of the nearly 100 basil plants we grew so that this book would have the correct botanical names of each species and variety. In Indiana, Dr. Simon and Mario Morales, an extraordinary plantsman and scientist, distilled the essential oils from the same plants so we could better understand the aromatic properties of our basils. Our friendship with these scientists over many years has been a valuable personal and intellectual asset.

The late Helen H. Darrah, through her seed collecting from the far corners of the world, and her writing, deserves much credit for bringing to public attention the vast array of basils available to the gardener. Her pioneering work, *The Cultivated Basils*, has been an inspiration for many gardeners and writers. Her detailed short history of basil was particularly helpful to us.

Growing 4,000 basil seedlings for our various research needs would not have been possible without the greenhouse help of Dottie Jacobsen, Laura Schneider, Rick Tagg, Francesco DeBaggio, and Amy Kocar. Deborah Hall played the part of a helpful wonder woman, growing basils, testing recipes, and baby-sitting during crucial stages of the research.

We want to thank especially the numerous friends and acquaintances in the herb business who helped in researching our basil biographies: Cy and Louise Hyde of Well-Sweep Herb Farm; Conrad Richter of Richters in Canada; Janika Eckert and Tricia Losornio of Johnny's Selected Seeds; Rosemary Nichols McGee of Nichols Garden Nurser; Madalene Hill, a gracious *grande dame* of the herb world; Peter Borchard of Companion Plants; and Kate Stadem, Beth Benjamin, and Wendy Krupnick of Shepherd's Garden Seeds. The following people went out of their way to give us personal assistance in collecting information and in locating basils. Richard Dufresne, Michael Soteriou, Chris and Popi Karamanos, and Giovanni Salvo.

A special tip of the hat to Joe Coca, Linda Ligon, and Judith Durant, the Interweave Press triumvirate that looks after our writing souls, irons out sentences, corrects our attitudes, illustrates our ideas, and makes everything look beautiful; and, of course, a big handshake to Karen Evanson who sees to it that absolutely everything else gets done. We especially appreciate Susan Wasinger's eye for design and attention to detail.

Our long-suffering spouses and children endured our basil breath, late night and early morning working hours, writers' blocks, long absences while in garden and greenhouse, distracting self-absorption, and experiments that ended on the dinner table —all this with good cheer and helpfulness. We owe them much for quietly indulging our dreams.

BASIL   An Herb Lover's Guide

Letters of Introduction

DEAR SUSAN: Put a cook and a gardener together with some basil and see what happens. I think this has book potential.

I foresee no problem playing the gardener's role in this horticultural drama; I've spent more than two decades making a living growing herbs and I have the part memorized. I dabble in the kitchen, but my feelings about recipes is, well, mixed, as you know. The American writer Henry Miller once wrote that when he heard the word "culture" he reached for his revolver; sometimes I have that feeling about "recipes". My favorite cookbook, *A Tuscan in the Kitchen*, lists ingredients but lacks amounts and cooking times. Guess that disqualifies me for the cook's part. Will you do the recipes?

You're a terrific gardener with a passion for basil, *and* you're a veteran of the cookbook wars. Your infectious enthusiasm would be a welcome counterpoint to me, often seen as an unsmiling curmudgeon with dirty knees. Best of all, your garden has lots of room to grow the dozens of basil varieties I can't squeeze into my cramped space. There are often ulterior motives to human activity and it's best to reveal them early, unless you're writing a murder mystery.

DEAR TOM: Hmm. Curmudgeon and Cook. Who better to write about basil? Basil has been my favorite herb since I was first introduced to it in its fresh form in Italy some twenty-plus years ago. I've grown many varieties and experimented with them in the kitchen. I think we share the same passion for basil. My first reaction is that this is a good idea. My second reaction is that we are going to have a great summer eating our way through the garden. Let's get to work.

DEAR SUSAN: Just a note to thank you for accepting my proposal to create some basil recipes and help me illuminate the basil garden. There is no doubt that Americans share our love for basil. I think it's the most popular herb in the nation. At my nursery, I sell more basil than anything else. In late April and early May, my greenhouse is a 2,000-square-foot basil plant factory. The way basil goes out of here, it makes me wonder why Americans have this summer obsession with basil and olive oil.

DEAR TOM: It's easy to imagine the source of this horticultural romance. Basil summons up warm summer evenings on a verandah somewhere in the Tuscan hills. It breathes warmth and sunshine into a dish in a sensual way unlike any other herb. Fresh summer basil is as basic and perfect as a succulent, ripe summer tomato at the peak of the season. It is the essence of summer's heat and it cannot be had at any other time of the year. This is what makes it so desirable.

DEAR SUSAN: What's always amazed me about basil is its diversity. Little leaves smaller than a postage stamp, big crinkled leaves the size of an adult's hand. Deep purple leaves with ruffles, or magic leaves of variegated green and purple. And the aroma! Cinnamon, anise, spicy cloves, lemon, and, of course, the indescribable traditional basil fragrance. It sometimes seems to me that a simple summer annual like basil, with such exciting diversity, can encompass the many faces and odors of the world. Is basil a metaphor for what's best in us?

DEAR TOM: Basil is beloved in many kitchens, it's true: its essential quality stimulates our senses and charms us. I believe smell is at least 50 percent of taste, which is why basil leads us by the nose into the kitchen. Elementary alchemy. Complex combinations of citrus and spice are blended with hints of anise and mint. One lemon basil lends itself to fish, while another offers a delightful fragrance that is refreshing in lemonade. Spicy clove basil will add mystery to a scone or to chutney, and cinnamon basil can be substituted for the spice in my grandmother's recipe for stewed tomatoes.

DEAR SUSAN: Good food is surely the reason why a cook would want the pleasure of fresh basil and to have it in a garden is almost essential. Basil is one of the easiest herbs to grow and it thrives on summer heat. But there are some cultural tricks, overlooked by many gardeners, which produce healthier and more productive plants.

Eating and gardening would be enough to ask of this world, but the complex universe of basil also holds excitement for me. Basil is an herb colored with a rich history and complex lore created from romance and mystery. It all adds up to the sweet, poetic power of basil to seduce the senses.

DEAR TOM: Practicality and romance, hummm? *Basil: A Treatise by Curmudgeon and Cook*. Beguiled by basil, two aficionados decide to join forces to explore the depth and range of the world of basil with the desire to somehow capture the essence of this alluring herb. We hope to inspire fellow gardeners and cooks with our findings—from cultivation and cultivars to sensory stimulation and kitchen magic.

History, Lore, and Uses

Mysteries and ghosts of the past still lurk

in the recesses of our gardens and in books.

—HELEN H. DARRAH, *The Cultivated Basils*

For more than 2,000 years, sweet, curvaceous basil leaves have been associated with images solemn and joyous, frightful and erotic. Such a diverse history befits a humble weed with a noble name and an aroma so intoxicating it makes the senses tingle with the adventure of every breath. This beautiful, varied plant has survived its checkered past to become the essence of the summer herb garden, gathering a large and devoted following that has made it a culinary icon. Tree tall or garden fairy short, with huge puckered leaves or tiny smooth ones, basil is more than a simple herb.

There are 30 to 150 basil species (depending on who's counting), and numerous cultivated varieties. A few basils are perennial in their native tropical habitats, but most are annuals, plants that die after flowering and producing seeds or fruits.

Botanists place basils in the *Ocimum* genus, part of the group called Lamiaceae (formerly Labiatae), a large amalgam of plants that are characterized by stems that are square in cross section and leaves that grow opposite each other as they climb the stem. Thyme, oregano, rosemary, lavender, and mints are other familiar herbs in this botanical family.

The botanical name for basil is *Ocimum basilicum*. The first name, the genus, comes from the Greek word *Okimon*, meaning smell. The species name, *basilicum*, is the Latin translation of the Greek word *basilikon*, meaning king. The English word "basil" is pronounced in several ways, providing a bit of controversy and an opportunity for heresy, a conundrum similar to whether "herb" is spoken "erb" or

This beautiful, varied plant has become the essence of the summer herb garden. Shown here is a basket of lettuce-leaf basils.

"herb". Is it "baysil" or "baaasil"? Both are common and correct. In much of the rest of the world, there is also plenty of basil cacophony. An Italian will understand *basilico*, but a French gardener grows *basilic*; the Portuguese have their *mangericao* and the Japanese know it as *bajiru*; the Dutch like their *bazielkruid*.

Basil leaves may be as small as a fingernail or as large as an open hand, and they are generally heart- or lance-shaped. The leaves on some varieties are smooth while others are hairy. They vary from green to purple with a wide range of mixtures of the two colors. The herb's aromatic subtleties are often surprising, and its considerable physical variety is prompted by its ability to hybridize across species lines—a salutary trait that not all plants enjoy. The aroma and taste of basil, often the feature that first captivates a cook or gardener, is enhanced by this promiscuous behavior. The genus' varied gene pool creates a plethora of clear, gem-like scents that range through lemon, camphor, cinnamon, clove, and anise.

The cause of basil's aromatic diversity is no secret. Basil is a little chemical factory, as are other herbs. It produces aromatic essential oils which are contained in microscopic sacs on various parts of the plant. When the plant is brushed or chewed, these sacs are ruptured, releasing some of the fragrant chemicals.

The flavor of basil is hard to define in simple words and is sometimes discussed by the cognoscenti as if it were a fine wine. However, acuity of the senses varies among individuals and is related to memory and experience. For true definition, specialized testing procedures make chemical typing of basil and other herbs so precise that, once a botanist has correctly identified specific varieties, they can be recognized by *both* chemistry and appearance.

In 1985, three Purdue University scientists analyzed the most popular basils in the United States to identify their main flavoring agents. James Simon and his associates Jim Quinn and Renée Murray found that the name "sweet basil" defines a group of cultivated varieties with medium to large leaves and specific but subtly different scents.

Chemical analysis of sweet basil reveals many compounds, but three—linalool, methyl chavicol, and eugenol—stand out as primary contributors to its signature aroma. Linalool, also a significant part of the aroma of lavender, provides the light floral character of many popular culinary basils. It constitutes from 7 to 59 percent of the essential oil in the many varieties of sweet basil. The varying amounts of methyl chavicol, also the basis of French tarragon's assertive flavor, gives the rich anise scent of some sweet basils. The friendly hint of clove in many basils derives from eugenol. As the percentage of these three chemicals shifts, the resulting aromas mark distinctive new sweet basil varieties. (The chemistry of many of the basils is discussed in Chapter 3.)

■ The origins of basil

Basil is native to Africa, Asia, the Middle East, the Caribbean, and South America, but it probably didn't arrive in Europe until a little more than 2,000 years ago. It is likely that early explorers and conquerors were drawn to basil not for its culinary uses, but for its ties to sacred rites and its alleged supernatural powers.

In *The Food of Italy*, Waverly Root writes that "basil was considered in antiquity as a sacred plant which was cut only with an instrument of some noble metal (iron was considered too base for this task) by a person who had previously performed purificatory rites, and in the absence of anyone in a state of impurity, for instance women during menstrual periods." It wasn't long after basil arrived in Rome that it became a part of Christian legend. During the reign of Emperor

Basil plants contain all the promise and joy any gardener may desire. Shown here is the garden of Mary Ruth and Neil Williams, Ft. Collins, Colorado.

Constantine (A.D. 306 to 337), the emperor's mother, Helena, is said to have had a divine revelation that led her to a basil patch where she found what she presumed were the remains of the cross on which Christ was crucified. This association turned basil into a ritual plant representing grief, redemption, and magic.

Italian traditions about basil also include the secular. Young women who pinned a basil leaf to their clothing were said to be proclaiming their chastity. On the other hand, a pot of basil set on a windowsill signified that a woman was ready to entertain her lover. Tuscans considered basil a plant with erotic powers.

The Greeks adopted basil, too. On St. Basil's Day, the first day of the new year, Greek women took basil to be blessed. "Upon returning home," Helen Darrah

The most stunning of Gerard's basils was a foot (30 cm) or more tall with a purple stem and large deeply cut purple leaves, perhaps similar to the modern variety, 'Purple Ruffles'.

writes in *The Cultivated Basils*, "the women strew some of the leaves upon the floor for good fortune, eat some with their families to insure health during the coming year, and more practically place the remaining leaves in chests to guard against mice and moths." Other Greek orthodox uses of basil expanded over Eastern Europe and eventually merged, Darrah believed, with Muslim traditions to spread basil lore in Northern Africa and Spain.

Some views of basil have been more disapproving. John Gerard, the sixteenth-century English writer and herbalist, quoted Galen, a second-century A.D. physician and writer on medicine and philosophy, who warned against the internal use of basil. Gerard followed that admonition with Dioscorides' belief that eating basil "dulleth the sight . . . breedeth wind, provoketh urine, drieth up milk." Gerard acknowledged that there were those in his time (circa 1597) who shunned basil because "if it be chewed and laid in the sun, it ingendreth worms." Flies and more serious pests where also on the list of evils caused by basil; it was believed that basil left under a stone for several days would turn into a scorpion. In 1653, Nicholas Culpepper summarized basil's medicinal uses and at the same time outlined the anxiety about the plant this way: "Being applied to the place bitten by venomous beasts, or stung by a wasp or hornet, it speedily draws the poison to it. *Every like draws its like*. Mizaldus affirms that being laid to rot in horse dung it will breed venomous beasts. Hilarius, a French physician, affirms upon his own knowledge that an acquaintance of his, by common smelling of it, had a scorpion breed in his brain."

Even in sleep, it was impossible to escape the presumed evil influence of basil. It was believed that dreams with any representation of basil in them would almost always end in the awakened dreamer's meeting misfortune or being tortured by unhappiness.

A less fearful view of basil began to appear in the early seventeenth century. John Parkinson, the botanist and royal apothecary to two English kings, offered a somewhat benign view of basil's virtues. He wrote in his 1629 *Paradisi in Sole Paradisus Terrestris* (found today under the anglicized title *A Garden of Pleasant Flowers*) that common basil was used to make "sweet or washing waters" and sometimes used in nosegays. Medicinally, the seed was used powdered "to procure a cheerful and merry heart."

Some of the early fear and loathing of basil may have been caused by a misreading of Greek. Basil was just an aromatic plant, but a basilisk was a fearful, fabled, lizard-like, fire-breathing monster. The Greek word for basil was *basilikon*; a basilisk was *basiliskos*. The Latin translations were also similar: *basilicum* (basil) and *basiliscus* (basilisk).

Despite the trepidation about basil, its roots took firm hold in Europe, especially in southern France and Italy where it may have been found as early as the second century B.C. Sweet basil and bush basil made their debut in England between 1548 and 1572, curiously not as a European import but from India. Spanish, Portuguese, French, and English colonists brought basil to the New World and it was found in the Massachusetts Bay Colony by 1621.

The varieties of basils available in late sixteenth- and early seventeenth-century England were described by Gerard and Parkinson. Modern gardeners may be surprised by how little the basil garden has changed. Gerard's mammoth compendium *The Herbal or General History of Plants* (1633 edition, revised by Thomas Johnson) lists four basil varieties. The most stunning of Gerard's basils was a foot or more tall with a purple stem and large "deeply cut" purple leaves (2 inches [5 cm] broad by 3 inches [7.5 cm] long) that he said were "thick and juicy." The branches end in "spokie tufts of white flowers with purple veins running alongst them." This plant was much like Burpee's 'Purple Ruffles', a 1987 All American Selection. Gerard also characterized a large green-leafed basil with "broad, thick and fat leaves, of a pleasant sweet smell"; some leaves "here and there are of a black reddish colour," he added. Another basil, smaller in stature and leaf size than the first two, had "a most odoriferous smell, not unlike the smell of a lemon . . . whereof it took his surname." Also mentioned was a low, many-branched, sweet-smelling, small-leafed "bush" or "fine" basil.

Parkinson covered much of the same territory, but added to Gerard's observations. According to Parkinson, lemon basil was England's "common basil"; the other two basils that he mentioned were "greater strangers in our country" and only "planted in curious gardens." A dwarf basil mentioned by Parkinson appears almost identical to Gerard's except that it was clove-scented. A purple basil similar to Gerard's had leaves that were "oftentimes a little crumpled", and its source was said to be the "West Indies".

During the early eighteenth century, botanists sailing aboard ships that were exploring the world returned to Europe with new plants and seeds to add to basil collections. French and English horticulturists named more than sixty basil varieties between 1780 and 1840. Richard Bradley reported in his 1726 book *New Improvements of Planting and Gardening* that he had received more than fifty basil varieties from the Grand Duke of Tuscany. By 1762, Carolus Linnaeus (Karl von Linne), the father of our plant classification system, had described eight basil species. By 1836, English botanist George Bentham had classified twenty-nine basil species and nine varieties of *O. basilicum*. In less than sixty years, John Isaac Briquet brought the total basil species count to forty-seven.

By the mid-twentieth century, the headlong fascination with basil that had marked the previous one hundred years had ebbed. Maude Grieve, writing *A Modern Herbal* in 1931 Britain, could comment that basil was no longer grown much there—understandably so—considering the cool, rainy environment and the bland British cooking habits. About the same time, the U.S. Department of Agriculture was growing a field of basil at its experimental farm in Arlington,

Virginia, to see if the crop could be produced in the United States. The plants did well, but the timing was premature. Sometime between 1964 and 1984, the department's statistics indicate that basil-mania hit America. During that period, basil imports grew from a measly 21 tons to 1,584 tons (19,000 kg to 1,437,000 kg) per year.

Today, the plant that was the target of harsh opinions during the Dark Ages is readily available at garden centers and through mail-order catalogs. Basil has been reborn in America and has reached an apotheosis in the contemporary culinary herb garden where it is grown for its aromatic ornamental leaves and its flowers. Basil flowers are carried in whorls around spikes of varying length; sometimes the spikes are clustered in shapes like cones or balls, making them lovely garden embellishments. Other short, mound-shaped basils are used for garden edging.

Commercial uses of basil abound. It is used in products that range from mouth-wash to medicine, from perfume (Brut) to liqueur (Chartreuse). Basil has reached the shelves of supermarkets, finding its way into baked goods, candy, gelatins, even ice cream. In the kitchen, basil is used to flavor soups, stews, vegetables, eggs, meats, poultry, seafood, rice, and salads. Zesty colored vinegars flavored with purple basils delight a cook's eyes.

Elsewhere in the world, where plants figure prominently in the pharmacopoeia, basil plays an important role. In West Africa, the herb is used for coughs and fevers. In eastern Africa, basil roots are boiled and leaves are chewed to alleviate stomachaches and colds. In India, gonorrhea is treated with basil, while Sudanese skin diseases are treated with a basil paste.

From East to West, essential oils are distilled from basil foliage and flowers, making the plant an important crop in Southern and Eastern Europe, Africa, India, and the Far East. European oils, which rely on sweet basils, are considered the finest and have a flowery, anise aroma. Réunion or Comoro basil oil is harsh-er, while basil oils from Bulgaria and Java have more exotic cinnamon and clove aromas.

New research suggests that basil has a bright future in a wide array of products from medicines to food flavorings to natural insecticides. A new cinnamon basil offers promise to the food industry where its easily extracted essential oil provides a low-cost substitute for the more expensive cinnamon bark. This cinnamon basil may also be important in fighting oral gum disease. *Ocimum suave*, a basil native to Kenya, may have a future protecting stored corn against pests. Essential oil extracts of basil may also be used to produce insecticides that kill mosquito larva, house flies, fleas, and fruit flies.

■ A history of pesto

While Americans are being swept off their feet by their new love affair with basil, the Italian's passion for this plant, especially its use in that creamy, perfumed green sauce called pesto, is the basis of a European culinary history that began before the Christian era.

Two ancient writers are considered the precursors of modern basil culture and gastronomy. Nearly 2,000 years ago, Pliny, the Roman naturalist and writer, provided farmers with instructions on planting, growing, and using basil; he advised them to feed the plant to their horses and asses to increase the beasts' fertility.

Writing with a poet's insight, Virgil more accurately saw the future of basil in the kitchen, not the stable. It is Virgil, the last great Roman poet of the pre-Christian era, who many Italians consider the father of pesto. Virgil is especially venerated by the Ligurians, denizens of that narrow, crescent-shaped piece of the Italian Riviera at the top of the western side of the Italian boot. They regard him as the first writer to mention pesto.

While Virgil is esteemed by Ligurian pesto fanciers and Pliny's words can be read today, their familiarity with basil has been called into question. Virgil certainly described a basic recipe for pesto, but he didn't specify basil as an ingredient, only herbs. Darrah points out in her monograph on basil that etymologists doubt Pliny had ever seen basil before he wrote about it. Further reservations are raised about European familiarity with basil at such an early date. In a modern translation of what may be the oldest known cookbook, the *De Re Coquinaria* of Apicius, twenty herbs familiar then and now are mentioned, but basil is not one of them. Yet, according to the translator, John Edwards, a Roman such as Apicius at the beginning of the Christian era would have had "access through Greek and Roman traders to the spice markets of southern Asia" as well as "the resources of North Africa, the Near East" and western Europe.

We know for sure that basil was firmly established on the Italian peninsula by the fourteenth century because Giovanni Boccaccio, Italy's wickedly ribald chronicler of upper class mores, immortalized the herb in one of the stories of his masterpiece, *The Decameron*. While the story details the murder and dismemberment of a woman's lover, Boccaccio reveals basil's commonplace role in the life of his times. He discloses that Italian gardeners of that era were so familiar with basil and its cultivation that they reserved large "handsome" pots especially for the herb. Gardeners and cooks of the time were sophisticated enough to distinguish different basil varieties; the best, they concluded, came from Salerno.

In *The Decameron*, Boccaccio discloses that Italian gardeners of that era were so familiar with basil and its cultivation that they reserved large "handsome" pots especially for the herb.

It is difficult to pinpoint when pesto arrived on Italian dinner tables. In her 1987 book, *Pasta Classica*, Julia della Croce says that pesto "is among the oldest known Italian dishes," and adds that the rich, green sauce probably came about through the "combined influences of Arabs, Persians, and Byzantines." Tradition, the final arbiter when historical fact is lacking, attributes the insinuation of basil into Western culture to Alexander the Great, king of Macedonia between 336 and 323 B.C.; the herb was a horticultural treasure brought by Alexander from Persia (Iran) after its conquest.

The first time the word "pesto" was used in a published work in English was 1937; a little more than a half century doesn't seem long for a foreign word to become common American usage. John Thorne described the Italian sauce in a small work devoted to garlic, oil, and basil as "a remarkable mix of fragrance and flavor, a bit salty, a bit sweet, a bit earthy."

As for the derivation of *pesto*, Piero Rebora, 1959 compiler of *Cassell's Italian-English Dictionary*, lists *pesto* as a word that means pounded, battered, bruised, and trampled upon. This translation certainly describes what basil leaves go through on their way to becoming pesto. Giuliano Bugialli, as savvy an interpreter of Italian cooking as we may have in the States, says in *The Fine Art of Italian Cooking* that "pesto of course refers to the pestle [*pestello* in Italian], as the grinding was originally done with that implement and a mortar." Does the word for the sauce come from the action or the instrument? Actually, both the Italian words *pesto* and *pestello* share the same Latin root, *pinsere*, which meant to pound.

The pesto tradition appears to have first settled in the Italian province of Liguria, an area with a rich history of cooking with herbs. From an early date, the business of the region was led by merchant traders and seafaring men. The Genoese, along with the Venetians, dominated the spice trade before it was seized by Portuguese in the late fifteenth century. It was on their long, deep water voyages that Genoese sailors "breathed day and night (rising through the hatches which covered their holds) the nauseating odors of pepper from India, cloves from Zanzibar, cinnamon from Ceylon, pimiento from the West Indies" according to Waverly Root in *The Food of Italy*. When the sailors returned home, Root says, they "found in its basil and garlic the green freshness and the earthy pungency they craved after their long odysseys," and they "wanted those qualities in strong, even exaggerated, form." It was in Liguria, with a cuisine shaped to the tastes of sailors homesick for fresh herbs, that the cult of basil, and its fondest offspring, pesto, took hold.

The original version of pesto may have been too robust for people who did not appreciate a sailor's life. The French have what Root calls a "local variant" of pesto which they call *pistou*, an altered artifact from the time when the Genoese presence was strong. It is not only the French who temper the potency of their Italian neighbors' sauce. "Almost every Ligurian town of any importance has developed its own variant of pesto," according to Root. Residents of Nervi, only seven miles from Genoa, smooth the rough edges of the traditional sauce by adding cream.

The historic pesto of Liguria consists of a local, sharp sheep cheese, olive oil, basil, and nuts mashed in a marble mortar with a wooden pestle to make a thick green sauce. The classic pesto of Genoa today is only slightly changed; parmesan was added to the recipe less than a hundred years ago. Here is Root's version:

The soul of *pesto* is basil, and the patience and care characteristic of Genoese cooking appear from the very start of pesto making in the meticulous preparation of the basil. It is first deprived of its stems and central veins; only the deveined leaves go into the mortar in which it will be ground. Pesto makers are adamant on this point: no one can chop the ingredients fine enough; they must be ground. . . . You begin by crushing the basil leaves carefully with coarse kitchen salt and a clove of garlic. The tender green color of this mixture is your guide for the rest of the process. It should be maintained as the other ingredients are added; if it weakens, put in more basil. Next you add equal parts of young Sardinian pecorino cheese and old parmesan (if you want a stronger taste, increase the proportion of the sharp Sardinian cheese; if you want it milder, decrease it). As you grind this with the rest, add olive oil (preferably Ligurian) drop by drop, until you have achieved the desired density (you may want it thicker for soup than pasta). The last ingredient is pine nuts (some persons use walnuts instead), which must be crushed so thoroughly that they become an indistinguishable part of the whole pungent creamy mass.

Bugialli concurs, generally, with Root's description of the Genoese version of the basil sauce. "The Genoese are wonderfully conservative about food, so that medieval and Renaissance dishes that have disappeared elsewhere still hang on in Genoa," he writes in *The Fine Art of Italian Cooking*. "Therefore, the making of pesto in Genoa is a rite and must be done with mortar and pestle." Bugialli believes nuts were part of the sauce from the beginning, not a later addition. "Nuts were commonly used in all green sauces of the Renaissance," he says.

Creeping revisionism has begun to challenge pesto traditionalism even in its hometown. Bugialli says "many of the old Genoese families" now "mix a little butter into the ingredients to be ground." Even parsley, to add a greener color, is finding its way into the pesto on some Ligurian dinner tables. Tuscans often substitute pancetta for the butter, and use a little cooked spinach to maintain the green color. A version of Tuscan pesto also contains ground peppercorns.

Pesto now belongs to the world, much to the chagrin of some Italians, and many variants are available. Thorne, in his essay *Aglio, Oglio, Basilico* (Garlic, Oil, Basil), describes the food fights over pesto among popular cookbook authors. Paula Wolfert offers a pesto recipe with 2 cups (480 ml) basil, 1/3 cup (80 ml) parmesan, 2½ teaspoons (13 ml) pecorino, 1/2 cup (120 ml) olive oil, 1/4 cup (60 ml) pine nuts, 2 garlic cloves, and 2 to 3 teaspoons (10 to 15 ml) heavy cream. Marcella Hazan's interpretation is close to Wolfert's, but instead of cream she recommends 3 teaspoons (15 ml) of butter. Bugialli suggests 3 cups (720 ml) of basil and 4 ounces (113 g) each of parmesan and sardo, 12 walnuts, 2 teaspoons (10 ml) of pine nuts, 3 garlic cloves, 4 teaspoons (20 ml) of butter, and 4 to 5 peppercorns. Julia Child, on the other hand, goes French; her pistou uses less basil, more garlic, and includes tomatoes. Child's sauce, which is thinner and less green than traditional pesto, is made with 1/4 cup (60 ml) basil, 1/2 cup (120 ml) parmesan, 1/4 to 1/2 cup (60 to 120 ml) oil, no nuts, 4 garlic cloves and 6 teaspoons (30 ml) of tomato puree. These are just some of the basil pesto variants in vogue.

Many pesto recipes, new and old, substitute mint, spinach, thyme, parsley, sage, cilantro, parsley, marjoram, borage, arugula, and even Swiss chard for basil. While it may seem scandalous to call a green sauce of thyme, spinach, or chives pesto, there is some precedent for it. Bugialli points out that pesto "is also related to the many types of salse verdi that one finds in old Renaissance cookbooks."

Much of the argument over what constitutes "real pesto" may involve subtle disputes over the quantities of each ingredient, but pesto lovers never tire of worrying the details to death; even the proper utensils for preparation are in contention. The traditional utensils of pesto making are the mortar and pestle through whose use the sauce evolves slowly so the cook may control its every nuance. Among traditionalists, there is even argument about how to use the pestle. For Bugialli, the pestle is an instrument of gentility, used "not to crush, but rather to push the ingredients in a circular motion against the stone." The method described by Francesco Solari to Molly O'Neill of *The New York Times Magazine* is anything but gentle. Solari and his wife, Melly, own *Ca' Peo Strada Panoramica*, a restaurant in the Ligurian hills that O'Neill says is "one of Italy's finest." Here's the way O'Neill describes Solari's pesto making: "Basil should never know a blade, Solari says. He is not sure why this is, just that hand-smashing brings out the best in the leaf. 'Pound, pound, pound!' he cries, moving his fist up and down on an invisible podium. . . . ."

In Bugialli's native Tuscany, the *mezzaluna,* a crescent-shaped, two-handled knife, is used to chop the pesto ingredients quickly. American pesto, on the other hand, is usually the product of high-tech kitchen equipment such as a food processor or a blender. But almost everybody agrees that the mortar and pestle produce the clearest, most intense flavors.

The sometimes contradictory advice about pesto often obscures the simplicity of the preparation process and purpose. Thorne has put this in clear perspective:

> The problem is that in pesto, as in many other recipes, there are variables beyond the control of the writer—basil has different intensities, cheeses (even of the same name) are bolder or tamer, and even your own palate changes from day to day. To compensate for all these factors, it is better to work not from a recipe, but from a sense of where you want to end up. This is a good rule in much cooking, but with pesto it is not even a difficult one.

Cookbook authors and historians are an opinionated lot, but they are mainly silent on the most important aspect of pesto—the specific basil variety to use. Of course, you can use any basil you choose, but not just any basil will produce the traditional pesto. Probably the closest you will come to the flavorful basil of Liguria is found in the United States under the names Genovese, Genoa Green, and Profumatissima.

However pesto is concocted, it is probably not going to be a regular visitor to the dinner tables of those on diets that restrict calories or cholesterol. Yet, rich as it is in cheese and olive oil, pesto is not just empty calories; the basil part of the sauce contains Vitamin C, calcium, and iron, but not in quantities that would lead anyone to mistake the plant for a vitamin bottle. The benefits of basil reside in its exquisite flavors and in knowing you are partaking in a small, but very old, tradition.

The inexorable rhythm of history has enveloped basil and its charming culinary offshoot, pesto. The cycle whose stages involve experimentation, acceptance, elevation to orthodoxy, then challenge and more experimentation has come full circle. As Italian food such as pizza and pesto has spread around the globe and been subjected to alterations in the name of commerce, convenience, and regional taste, traditionalists have organized to prevent the dilution of the classical cuisine. In Naples, a movement is underway to classify pizza much like fine wine and prevent outrageous variants from carrying the pizza label. In Genoa, the *Confraternita del pesto*, an association founded in 1992, has become the official watchdog of basil traditionalism. Not only does the organization serve as a repository of information and history, it has encouraged basil producers from the traditional growing areas of Pra, Pegli, Coronata, Palmaro, and Voltri to designate their packets of fresh basil leaves with a tag that reads, "Basilico di Genova", the first move toward a *denominazione di origine controllata e garantita*, an appellation, or grading standard, that for the elite of fresh basil is a guarantee of quality and trueness to type similar to that given to the finest Italian wines.

Basil has been produced in Genoa for centuries, but it wasn't until the late 1920s, when greenhouse production began, that the perfumed herb was available year-round. Greenhouse basil is now available for ten months; during the summer when field production is at its peak the greenhouse soil rests.

A special method used to grow and harvest basil in the greenhouses may provide a key to the secret of Genoese pesto. Seed is sown inside the greenhouse in 8-foot (2.5-m) wide beds filled with a loose, well-drained medium amended with rice hulls. The harvest begins in thirty to forty days, as soon as seedlings have four leaves and two to four smaller leaves emerging from the stem tip. It is not unusual to see men balanced on sagging 2×8 (5×20) planks bending over these seedling beds to pull the young plants, along with their roots. After the plants are harvested, they are bunched, roots and all, and placed in moisturized plastic packets to keep them from wilting. A packet of fifty to sixty seedlings will provide pesto for a family dinner, and sells for a price that most Americans would consider high. The basil variety, the method of cultivation, the timing of the harvest, and the handling afterwards play essential roles in the quality of any basil used for pesto. With so many variables, it is clear that the best basil for the sauce is that which is grown and picked by the cook in a garden close by the kitchen door, or closer. (See page 47 for a method of growing basil indoors.)

The history of pesto reflects the notion that the personality of an epoch is expressed in small things as well as large. Food is one of the most important talismans to explore in understanding history. Pesto arose in an era of strict adherence to tradition, the opposite of the style of our time which emphasizes individuality. It is the tension between these two conflicting ideas that fuels the pesto debate. What is clear is that a cook's experience, instinct, taste, and indi-

viduality play pivotal roles in making pesto, whether it is created along traditional or modern lines.

As we all realize sooner or later, the past is often rediscovered quietly residing
in the present, but gardeners, especially those who seek the unusual and wondrous, seem bedeviled by a compulsion to plant something "new" that has been
around for centuries. Basil in contemporary American gardens is emblematic of
this urge, but at least we have overcome the fears and traditions of the Middle
Ages. Basil hasn't given birth to scorpions for some time, and it has helped another former outcast, the tomato, survive in mutual admiration. It is satisfying to find
justice in a place as useful as the garden. For basil, a little knowledge and sanity,
plus imagination fueled by an alluring aroma, has rescued what had been a sacred,
feared plant, and transformed it into a modern herb of gustatory delight.

Basil Cultivation

Surely that ground is best of all other,

which hath an aromaticall smell and taste with it.

—PLINY, *Pliny's Natural History*

So much has happened to horticulture in the last 2,000 years that few gardeners seek the advice of Pliny anymore. Born in the second decade of the Christian era, this Roman naturalist and writer advised basil growers to curse and stamp the earth as the seeds were scattered in the field. The foul incantations and violent motions were believed to bring forth supernatural forces which would improve germination and growth. Perhaps, too, they were meant to solidify the preeminence of the gardener in the magical process of gardening in which so much has always been left to chance.

Fortunately, we no longer have to depend on incantations to release the once-mysterious energies of basil seeds. We now understand that seeds are dormant, living embryos awaiting the moisture that will awaken them to growth and reproduction. However, it would be as much a mistake today as it was in Pliny's time to reduce the cultivation of basil to a simple set of instructions. Gardening is more than mere exploitation; it involves having a romance with the earth as much as it does growing good things to eat.

If you carefully inspect a thick basil flower spike after all the blossoms have dropped, you will see the remarkable way nature has packaged the next generation of plants. Basil blooms in rings around the flower stem from structures called calyxes. The ring closest to the ground often blooms first. The stems vary in length and shape; some are long and angular, while others are short, with many compressed branches that create ball or cone shapes.

Inside each of the flowers that ring a basil stem are four ovaries. When fertilized, the ovaries become seeds, more accurately designated as nutlets; these can be seen easily if the flower stem is held upside down. Each set of nutlets hugs the other so tightly that they make an almost square, light ocher package. As the nutlets mature they become a blue so dark it appears black, or in some species, brown.

It takes 15,000 to 50,000 seeds to make an ounce (30 g) (depending on the variety and the seed company doing the counting). Smooth, oval basil seeds hold a surprise for the gardener who sows them inside in uncovered rows. A few minutes after being dampened with water, the dark seeds lighten to a soft pale blue and their hard exteriors become sticky and gelatinous. Pliny was right about the incantatory part of growing basil: so humble in their dark carapaces, the seeds are almost magical in the way they spring to life. At that moment of emergence, the basil seedlings contain all the promise and joy any gardener may desire.

∎ What cultural conditions do you need?

Basil's needs are few but they are important, and a gardener preparing to grow this annual herb must pay close attention to those needs if success is to follow. The semi-tropical and tropical areas of the world to which *Ocimum* species are native offer some obvious clues to their cultural needs—warm, sunny weather and plenty of moisture. Specifically, basils do well where hot-weather vegetables such as tomatoes, peppers, and eggplants flourish; their finest growth occurs during periods when night temperatures are above 60°F (15°C). Thus, in most areas of the United States, basil has a limited period of rapid growth. In the mid-Atlantic area, where we live, basil grows well for only about 140 days, beginning in late May or early June and ending in October.

Three basic parameters of basil cultivation—precipitation, temperature, and soil pH—were outlined in 1982 by James A. Duke, then an economic plant specialist for the U.S. Department of Agriculture. His report shows that *Ocimum basilicum*, the most common culinary species of basil, grows with as little as 11 inches (28 cm) and as much as 169 inches (430 cm) of rain annually. The temperature swings that this sweet basil withstands are considerable—46° to 84°F (8° to 29°C), as are the pH readings (4.3 to 9.1). These three environmental factors bracket outdoor cultivation possibilities, but do not define optimum conditions.

While the extremes are important to know, it is the mean values of temperature, pH, and precipitation that are closer to the optimum growing conditions, Duke believes. That would put the ideal place to grow basil in a climate with a temperature of about 65°F (15°C), with soil pH of 6.6, and annual precipitation of about 53 inches (135 cm). Since soil pH and moisture are easily modified in the garden, the chief limiting factor to outdoor basil cultivation is temperature. But even that factor has surprising flexibility.

Unable to greenhouse the basil collection amassed for this book, Tom decided to leave the plants outside to test cold hardiness. The experiment actually masked his true motivation: softening the blow of final disposal. After several nights of temperatures below freezing had blackened the basil leaves and left them crisp, Tom began the chore of final accounting. As he cut the defoliated stems of holy basil (*O. tenuiflorum*), he saw that they still contained life in their green cores. These natives of warm India had performed against logic and withstood temperatures that had killed other basils. He took the sacred Hindu plants into the greenhouse, and within a few weeks their bare stems sprouted leaves.

Gardeners who approach their little plots with an adventurous spirit and watch their plants with a knowledgeable eye always learn something valuable, and it is often the failures that teach them the most.

■ How many plants do you need?

Gardeners and cooks calculate their basil needs differently, but the decision almost always comes down to appetite and space. After several years of growing basil, the experienced gardener knows what worked last year and adds plants as necessary. The new gardener, however, has no history to consult, no idea how many leaves to expect. Unfortunately, little information about basil plant yield is available to the home gardener; most data has been gathered for commercial producers. So we set out to find some answers by growing several popular varieties and harvesting them on a regular basis.

In addition to yield, there were a number of other things that we wanted to know about our basils. Would plants in pots filled with soilless growing medium perform differently from those grown in good garden soil? What disease problems could occur and how would they affect yields? Does leaf size influence the total weight of the harvested foliage? So many environmental factors influence basil yields that we hope you don't consider our data unchallengeable; use it as a guide and adjust to your specific gardening conditions.

We started by selecting ten culinary basil varieties: 'Piccolo verde fino', 'Red Rubin', 'Purple Ruffles', lemon, 'Genoa Green', 'Napoletano', 'Greek', 'Lesbos', 'Anise', and Thai. We transplanted well-branched basils from 6-inch (15-cm) pots into 12-inch (30-cm) containers, planting two containers of each variety in case a backup became necessary. We then transplanted basils of each variety into the garden, allowing a backup there, too.

We harvested thirty-two plants immediately after transplanting (the slow-growing purple-leaved basils took a month to reach the harvesting stage). Harvesting involved cutting each stem just above the pair of leaves at its base. We took the foliage cut from each plant indoors, removed the leaves from the stems without deveining them, and weighed them. Subsequent harvests were based on the growth of each variety and were made prior to flower-bud initiation. (Flowers occur on basil after each stem has a certain number of leaves; for details see the individual listings beginning on page 68.) Potted lemon basils were harvested six times between July 9 and October 16, while the slower growing potted 'Purple Ruffles' basil were harvested only three times during the same period.

It is commonly believed that basils with large foliage produce more volume and weight than those with small leaves. This notion was challenged by a comparison of the summer harvest from large-leaved 'Purple Ruffles' and the small-leaved lemon basil. With three harvests, the 'Purple Ruffles' produced nearly 11 ounces (310 g) of foliage. With six harvests, the lemon basil yielded 14.5 ounces (410 g). Harvested five times, the large-leaved Napoletano yielded a total of 19 ounces (540 g). These figures suggest that rapid growth and frequency of harvest may be more important factors than leaf size in determining a basil plant's yield.

Our second discovery was that there is virtually no difference between the yield of a basil plant grown in the garden and one grown in a container filled with a soilless growing medium. What is important in basil cultivation is well-drained soil and plant access to nutrients.

Disease, we learned, is the most unpredictable and damaging element in the garden environment, and its presence can substantially alter the amount of foliage obtained from a single plant. Half our test plants were so debilitated by shoot blight that data from them was useless. Both of the garden-grown 'Genoa Green' basils, for instance, were severely weakened by disease; their average foliage yield was only 8.5 ounces (240 g). The healthy pot-grown 'Genoa Green' produced an average of 27.5 ounces (780 g).

The weight of the foliage was the easiest way for us to determine yields, but since few cooks in America measure by weight, we packed 1 cup (240 ml) with whole 'Genoa Green' basil leaves, stems removed. One cup of foliage weighed 1.8 ounces (51 g).

The average amount of foliage produced by our test plants from the first harvest, July 9, through the last harvest, middle of October, was 13 ounces (369 g) or about 7 cups (1680 ml) of leaves per plant. 'Genoa Green' was the top foliage pro-ducer with 15 cups (3600 ml) of leaves; 'Purple Ruffles' was the lowest producer with 6 cups (1440 ml).

■ Ground work

Few untempered soils outside the soft, dark soils of the American Midwest meet basil's demanding standards for tilth and drainage. The rest of us, faced with heavy clay that holds few nutrients and can be as hard as a brick or with loose sandy soils that lack the ability to hold any nutrients, had best gather our tools and do a little ground work.

Like many herbs, basil is adaptable. Its best site is one with day-long sun, but most basil varieties will subsist on as little as three to four hours of direct sunlight. The plant is accommodated by a wide range of soil conditions, but will offer supe-rior growth in a well-drained, loamy soil that has a near-neutral pH (6 to 6.5) and is well-endowed with nutrients. Good air circulation is also necessary.

Begin soil preparation early in the spring, or late in the fall when weather is still nice and planning can be done in the absence of high-season pressures. Whether you hanker for a few square feet (1 sq. m) of basil or something much grander, the first step is to clear the sod and loosen the top 12 inches (30 cm) of soil with a shovel or spading fork. Add 4 to 6 inches (10 to 15 cm) of compost or sphagnum peat and mix thoroughly to obtain a soft, clod-free growing medium. An inch or two (2.5 to 5 cm) of manure along with an organic or inorganic fertilizer that con-tains nitrogen, phosphorus and potassium in either granular form or slow-release pellets may also be dug into this now-raised area. In parts of the country where soils are acidic, the pH should be raised by adding lime in proportions recom-mended by the local USDA extension office; soils with excessively high pH require the addition of sulfur to acidify them. Soil preparation, once performed, need not be an annual strain; the initial preparation should provide your basils with a beneficent Mother Earth, one that will offer the potential of big harvests for many years with the addition of a small amount of nutrients annually.

■ Growing basil from seed

Most basil species are produced from seed, although the occasional cultivar is so unstable (purple-leaved types are notoriously difficult for breeders to tame) that it must be reproduced through stem cuttings. The advantage of growing your own basil, rather than buying plants from a garden center or herb specialist, is the wide variety of types from which you have to choose. Seeds for a number of the more unusual types of basil are often not available in quantities required by commercial growers but may be bought by individuals. Also, space often limits even a specialist's desire to have a large array of basil varieties. If you are familiar with growing vegetable plants or ornamental annuals, it may seem that nothing could be easier than buying a packet of basil seeds and scattering a few in the garden. This is not a certainty with basil seeds sold in the United States. The plants that you get may leave you leaning against your spade in wonder. The certainty that your seed is viable and true to name is not yet as high with basil as it is with marigolds, petunias, or tomatoes.

In her 1980 monograph, *The Cultivated Basils*, Helen Darrah wrote, "many seed samples I have grown over a period of twenty-five years were mislabeled or produced plants which did not correspond to the descriptions of the species or the variety." In the mid-1980s, Dr. James E. Simon of Purdue University expressed the same frustration with seed variability. After spending three years testing basil varieties, Simon concluded, "Stricter quality control on seed purity and trueness to type as well as seed vigor of basil varieties and other culinary herbs is needed. Basic information such as germination percentage should be included on every herb seed packet, as this alone would aid in ensuring minimum seed viability and improve the performance that commercial growers and home gardeners expect."

If our sampling of the trade is a good indicator, the problems found by Darrah and Simon still exist. We purchased seed packets for eighty named basils from more than a dozen suppliers (some seeds we thought would be duplicates based on their names), but we were hardly prepared for what we got. Overall, 16 percent of the plants the seed produced were not what the packets described; one firm had mislabeled half their basil seed. We also found the same bush basil variety sold under five different names. On the other hand, one packet labeled 'Green Bush' produced a large-leaved sweet basil. A packet with a picture of a large, puckered-leaved basil labeled 'Green Ruffles' produced a tall, very small-leaved French basil. Another company's packet produced 'Green Ruffles' instead of the dwarf, small-leaved 'Green Bouquet' its label led us to expect. The most egregious labeling error came in a packet called 'Holy Basil.' The seed that it contained produced a tall, inedible, gangly plant we haven't been able to identify; according to Arthur O. Tucker of Delaware State University, it was not a basil of any type.

We were well aware that it is impossible to tell from the appearance of a basil seed what variety it will produce; this feature compounds the problem for seed merchants who must trust the word of their suppliers. Even with less than a perfect performance by some, we know that most seed companies are concerned about quality and accurate labeling. However, we believe that agreement on varietal names would help assure that gardeners receive the basils they believe they have ordered.

■ Sowing basil seed indoors

Basil can be sown directly in the garden. However, as with tropical vegetables such as tomatoes, peppers, and eggplants, it is ideally started from seed sown indoors four to six weeks before transplanting. The gardener who produces transplants has two important advantages over those who sow directly in the garden. Transplants provide a six- to eight-week head start over direct-sowing; this leads to earlier maturity and permits at least two additional harvests. In climates with less than two months during which nights are above 60°F (15°C), starting seeds indoors is necessary to obtain any harvest at all. The only drawback to starting your own seedlings is the need for some special equipment and space to use it.

Tabletop seed starting works well whether you want dozens of plants or only a few, but it is important to understand that indoor gardening takes time and attention. You need to provide the seeds and seedlings with perfect conditions for germination and growth. This calls for the knowledgeable manipulation of the essential ingredients of plant sustenance (soil, nutrients, light, temperature, and moisture). In a way, the gardener becomes a surrogate Mother Nature.

Basil dotes on sun and warmth from its seedling stage through maturity. It is not difficult for the indoor gardener to provide the necessary warmth and light for plant development, but it will require a small investment and some space. Natural light entering the typical home is insufficient to produce compact seedling growth; even the amount of light reaching seedlings in a greenhouse during the typical early spring period may be inadequate because of short day lengths and cloudy, rainy weather. The hardware for a seed propagation area consists of three essentials: a 24-hour timer capable of turning electricity off and on, fluorescent light fixtures with ordinary cool white or warm white tubes (expensive grow lights are unnecessary), and a plastic sheet to protect the surface on which the flats and pots sit. The ideal location for the lights has daytime temperatures to of at least 65°F (18°C) (the lights themselves will add about 10°F [5°C] to the ambient air temperature); nighttime temperatures may fall to 50°F (10°C).

The size of the fixtures will vary with the number of plants you want to produce. To determine space for the seedlings, use the following figures. Four hundred plants can be grown from seedlings germinated in a 10 by 20-inch (25 by 50-cm) plastic flat. A 5 by 5-inch (13 by 13-cm) pack is large enough to produce about fifty basil transplants. When these seedlings are transplanted to 2.5-inch (6-cm) pots, the space needed jumps to a little more than 24 square feet (7 sq m). A single two-tube, 4-foot-long (1.2 m) light fixture is adequate if not more than thirty-two plants in 2.5-inch (6-cm) pots are desired; up to sixty-four plants will be accommodated by two fixtures placed side by side. Rig the side-by-side lights so that the top edge of the fixture closest to you is 10 to 11 inches (25 to 28 cm) from the far edge of the fixture farthest from you; fixtures without reflectors are easier to place this close together. Wire the two fixtures in a series to allow them to work from a single plug. Chains attached to the fixtures provide height flexibility whether they hang from a basement ceiling, a clothes pole in a closet, or under a work table. The ability to move the light source up and down will be useful as the seedlings develop and later get transplanted into taller containers. When you're ready to begin growing your basil seedlings, plug your lights into a timer set so that the seedlings receive sixteen hours of artificial light daily.

The container in which you sow your seed needs special consideration. Pots of all sorts of shapes and materials may be used to start seedlings, but they must be sterile if they have been used previously; you're better off starting with virgin plastic. Whatever container you choose, be certain that it has drainage holes in the bottom. The depth of the container is more important than it may appear at first; if it is too deep the starting mix may remain wet too long and lead to damping off, a disease that causes the seedling's stem to rot at the soil line. The best container depth is between 1½ and 2 inches (4 and 5 cm); a high-sided container filled much below the top will block air from flowing over and through the seedlings and increase the risk of disease. Favorite containers of many seed starters are new 2-inch-square (5-cm-sq) plastic pots; nonpartitioned 5 by 5-inch (13 by 13-cm) plastic packs; 10 by 10-inch (25 by 25-cm) plastic flats; and 10 by 20-inch (25 by 50-cm) plastic flats.

Readily available commercial soilless mixes provide excellent, predictable results; garden soils require pasteurization to kill diseases and insects. The soilless mixes combine a variety of materials: sphagnum peat or composted bark for water retention, an equal amount of aggregates such as perlite (silica that is heated and expanded to 1400°F [760°C]), and vermiculite (an inert and sterile material made from mica that has been heated to 2000°F [1093°C]). An alternative seed-starting medium is vermiculite without any peat; perlite is rarely used by itself for seed starting because it is large and unable to hold nutrients in reserve. Propagation media should be dampened before seeds are sown. Peat-based media is sometimes difficult to wet; hot water can help. Too much moisture can cause seeds to rot. The media should be moistened just enough so that it is darkened but remains crumbly. If vermiculite is used, dampen it with a weak solution of liquid fertilizer (half the strength recommended on the label) and use the same solution to water seedlings once they emerge. (Purple basil seed sown in vermiculite, even with daily fertilization, often produces seedlings with washed-out leaf color, but strong pigment returns once they are transplanted.)

■ When to sow

Some planning is necessary before you sow the first seed. First determine the date you plan to transplant the seedlings into the garden. Then count back five to six weeks to determine the date to sow the seeds indoors. Five to six weeks will give the seeds time to germinate in flats, get transplanted into pots, and grow large enough to become garden-ready.

Seeds should be sown in rows and spaced so that there is about a seed-width between each one. Precision is not essential; fine seedlings can be produced even when seeds are piled upon each other. Space rows 1 to 2 inches (2.5 to 5 cm) apart so that air can circulate freely between the seedlings. It is not necessary to cover basil seeds with growing medium when they are sown indoors. After sowing, lightly water the pot or flat using a delicate touch so the starting mix does not cover the seeds (the hose spray at the kitchen sink is perfect). Then place the container in a transparent plastic freezer bag or cover it with plastic wrap taped to the sides of the container.

Choose a warm room for seed germination, but do not permit sunlight to hit the covered seedlings; it can cook the plastic-covered seeds and kill them. Heat mats are unnecessary as long as room temperatures remain between 65 to 70°F (18 to 21°C), a range warm enough for most basil seeds to germinate in three days.

Check for seed emergence each day. As soon as the first stirring of life is apparent, remove the plastic covering and move the seedling container to the light garden, which is usually in another space. Seedlings should be placed 2 to 3 inches (5 to 7.5 cm) below the fluorescent lights and usually need no water their first day under lights. Ideally, irrigation will commence the second day, but don't rush the process.

Water is a mixed blessing to plants, especially nascent basils. While it is necessary for the life of seedlings, not much more than small columns of water themselves, the roots also need the air contained in the rooting medium. If the water that fills the medium's air pockets is not taken up quickly or lost through evaporation, the seedlings may die from root rot.

The biggest error that first-time seed starters make is overwatering. Basil seedlings have a proclivity to keel over rapidly if kept too wet and the careful gardener will resist the temptation to water before it is time. Allow growing medium to dry between irrigations, but not to the point that the seedlings are stressed. (As peat-based starting media dry, they change from dark to light, making it easy to determine irrigation scheduling.) Whatever medium you use, apply the amount of water necessary to moisten it for a single day. If environmental conditions do not allow rapid drying of the medium, a fan blowing gently across the seedlings will accelerate transpiration.

Proper timing of seedling irrigation also creates healthy plants. The best method is to water soon after the lights have been turned on; this allows immediate water uptake and rapid evaporation. Watering just before the dark period causes seedlings to sit in water and may prove unhealthy.

When it is time to irrigate your basil seedlings, run tepid tap water into a watering can and apply it with the least damage to tender seedling growth. A gentle flow of water directed between the rows is ideal. Be careful not to overwater or cover the seedlings with starting medium. You'll know when you've overwatered because the growing medium will not be dry the next day. If this happens, water less next time. A solution of liquid fertilizer mixed at the rate recommended on the container should be used at least once a week with peat-based growing media, and at each irrigation with vermiculite.

About two to three weeks after germination, seedlings will have developed their first set of true leaves. This signals that they are ready to transplant. Use 2- or 2.5-inch (5- or 6-cm) plastic pots filled with a soilless growing medium; several seedlings may be combined in a clump and transplanted as one. Clump transplanting reduces root damage and transplant shock; with the clump taken all at once, the seedlings continue uninterrupted growth and are less apt to become diseased. Transplanted clumps are not separated later and produce a vigorous multistemmed plant that provides more foliage per square inch (2.5 cm) of garden than a single-stem plant.

Keep the potted seedlings under indoor fluorescent lights for two to three weeks to establish good root growth. Follow the same principles of irrigation as

Top: Cut stems about 4 inches long with a clean, sharp pair of scissors.
Bottom: Strip the leaves from the lower half.
Right: Put the cutting in a cup filled with enough water to cover only the bare stem.

used for emerging seedlings. Watering may be more infrequent at first because the pots hold more water in relation to the roots. Continue to fertilize every seventh irrigation.

■ Growing basil from cuttings

Any basil can be grown from a stem tip cutting, but not every basil can be grown from seed. At least three handsome, unusual basils that fall into the cutting-only category are 'Lesbos', 'Holly's Painted', and 'African Blue'. In addition, many purple-leaved basils show unusual variegations that you may want to preserve through cuttings.

Rooting basil cuttings is easy and quick to do in a cup of water and it costs virtually nothing. Styrofoam cups about 3 inches (7.5 cm) high are perfect for the job, and you can write identification on their sides; short glasses or jelly jars also work well. It's important to take cuttings from the tips of nonflowering stems on plants in vigorous growth; cuttings from plants growing in full sun root best. Cuttings from plants grown indoors or without enough sun are less likely to root well. Choose plants for cuttings that are both disease and bug free.

Cut stems about 4 inches (10 cm) long with a clean, sharp pair of scissors, then strip the leaves from the lower half. Fill the cups with water so that only the bare stems are immersed. About three or four cuttings will fit in a cup or glass without too much crowding. Put the cups with their cuttings on a windowsill that receives plenty of light; direct sun is not essential.

Once your cuttings are rooted, plant them in 2- to 3-inch (5- to 7.5-cm) pots, one cutting per pot.

The only trick to rooting cuttings in water is to change the water daily to prevent bacteria and diseases that cause stem rot. Daily changing also helps maintain the oxygen levels important to producing roots. Purple basil cuttings root a bit slower than their green sisters; most cuttings should be rooted well enough for potting in a week or two.

There is a notion that roots formed in water are weaker than those created in soil, or that they aren't "real roots", but this is something of a myth. In *Plant Propagation Principles and Practices*, an often-used textbook, Hudson T. Hartmann and Dale E. Kester, both of the University of California, actually list water as an acceptable medium for rooting "easily propagated species". Basil certainly fits that description.

Once your cuttings are rooted, plant them in 2- to 3-inch (5- to 7.5-cm) pots, one cutting per pot. If you've only rooted a single cutting, use the Styrofoam cup. Punch three holes in the bottom for drainage, then use a soilless growing medium. Place the potted cuttings in the sunniest spot in a greenhouse or under double-tube fluorescent lights to grow for a week or two. Adjust the lights so they are 2 to 3 inches (5 to 7.5 cm) above the potted cuttings. Care for cuttings under lights as for transplanted seedlings.

■ Transplanting to the garden

When seedlings and cuttings are ready to transplant, accurate timing and close attention to weather conditions are essential to provide the rousing start that will lead to bountiful harvests. Seedlings or cuttings grown under lights have very tender leaf tissue that is easily damaged by harsh cold and burning sun. A transition period is necessary to bridge the protective conditions indoors and the rough, take-it-as-it-comes environment outdoors. This period is called hardening off.

Timing the perfect day to transplant a persnickety herb such as basil is difficult; spring is like a puppy, predictably unpredictable and full of unanticipated antics every day. Seedlings transplanted outside before temperatures have sufficiently warmed the soil will usually dawdle and may be set back or stunted and offer low yields. As a rule of thumb, basil transplants should be set outside when spring's tantrums have stopped, the weather is settled, and no frosts are anticipated; this usually corresponds to the time eggplants are transplanted.

Cold frames help tender transplants through the transition to the harsh, real world. Their side walls protect plants from stiff breezes and their lids provide protection at night from sudden chills, but plants hardened off in cold frames do need overhead protection from the sun for four or five days. A simple inexpensive cardboard box filled with potted seedlings may substitute for a traditional cold frame.

Place the box in a position where the plants only receive sun before 10 a.m. If temperatures are predicted to dip below 50°F (10°C), bring the box indoors. After three or four days outdoors, ease the box into full sun; two days later transplant your basils to the garden.

Breathable, poly-garden fabric is another alternative to a cold-frame. This cloth-like material allows some light and water to penetrate, but is so lightweight it can be thrown over potted transplants or plants already in the garden to protect them from sun or cold. It can add as much as 5 to 10°F (3 to 5.5°C) to the air temperature around plants at night; double layers are especially effective. Hot caps, dome-like structures with open tops, provide protection from wind and cold and are handy where short seasons call for risky, early planting. Walls O' Water, pleated plastic devices filled with water that encircle new transplants, are also useful for cold protection.

Site your basil plants where they will receive sun all day, or at least 4 hours after 10 a.m.

Site your basil plants where they will receive sun all day, or at least 4 hours after 10 a.m. Plants should be spaced 12 to 18 inches (30 to 46 cm) apart; for the larger ornamental basils such as 'African Blue' and camphor, up to three feet (one meter) may be necessary between plants. When the transplants are set, put some water soluble fertilizer in the watering can before giving them the traditional drink that settles the dirt around the roots. Don't hesitate to irrigate basils as needed throughout the summer; as tropical plants they respond to heat and humidity, but should not dry out as rosemary, lavender, or tarragon can do. A fortnightly draft of liquid nutrient will bring amazing results in plant productivity.

■ Sowing seed outdoors

Direct sowing of basil seed in the garden has many advocates, especially when dozens of plants are desired. The procedure is simple and uncomplicated, but the risks are greater because the gardener has less control over the environment than indoors. Soil quality and high night temperatures are important factors for the germination and growth of seedlings started in this fashion. Proper soil moisture is a third necessity. Basil seed "if it be sown in rainy weather," cautioned Gerard in *The Herbal*, "will putrefy . . . and come to nothing." That is still good advice.

The basil seed bed should be smooth and without clods. Not only is warm soil important to germination, the ambient air that greets the emergent seedling had better be warm, too. Soil and air temperatures should be 55°F (13°C) or more at night, and the last possible frost date must be passed.

Seed sown too early will be greeted by damp spring ground and may rot. With air temperatures much below 55°F (13°C), the young plants may become stunted and stop growing, like peppers and eggplants under similar conditions. Seed sown outdoors, even under the best conditions, may take twice as long to germinate as seed sown indoors because temperature fluctuations are difficult to control. Outdoor seedlings will also grow more slowly for the same reason.

There are several ways to alter the natural environment for seed sowing. The soil set aside for basil can be warmed by placing a sheet of black plastic over it a week before seeding. After sowing, a layer of poly-garden fabric will hold warmth, allow moisture to penetrate the seed bed, and prevent birds and other seed-eating predators from disturbing the bed.

Once minimum temperatures are reached, scratch a row about 1/8-inch (3-mm) deep in the smooth soil and distribute the seeds so that they are close together but don't touch; cover lightly and water. Thereafter, water regularly so the dirt around the seeds doesn't completely dry out (remember that the soil surface dries first and what is underneath may still be wet for some time.) It will take five to fifteen days for seedlings to emerge; the warmer the temperatures, the more rapid the germination.

Soon after the seedlings emerge, the culinary fun can begin. The first leaves on the seedlings are D-shaped nurse leaves that are shortly replaced by more typical lance-shaped foliage. As soon as the seedlings present their first or second set of true leaves, it's time to start thinning. What you want eventually are small clumps of four or five basils that can grow into tall, beautiful plants. For starters, instead of removing all the seedlings between the clumps, pull the largest of the seedlings at random and leave the small ones to grow for later thinning. These large young seedlings are what the Genoese love to use for pesto, so they should go immediately to the kitchen, then to the table. Thin seedlings until the clumps stand 12 to 18 inches (30 to 46 cm) apart; now it won't be long until regular leaf harvests begin. Purple basils often begin to show variations in seedling leaf color early in life. When it comes time to thin them, pick seedlings that are not all purple.

■ Container culture

There is something so charming about basil plants that it is hard to ignore the urge to pot them and grow them on a sunny patio, balcony, or other spot. Gardeners have been bowing to this horticultural imperative since at least the 1300s, a testament to the plant's adaptability and people's fondness for it.

Anyone who has grown potted basils knows how beautiful and unusually decorative they can be. Purple basils make stunning accent plants, good in groupings or alone on a patio. For a really unusual decorative effect on a large balcony or patio, try a tub of 'African Blue' basil (O. 'African Blue'); it might reach three or four feet high in a single season. Similar in height, the stately, woody-stemmed 'East Indian' basil is another standout potted plant. The super tall 'Green' basil, growing head high in a single season, is also a conversation piece.

As for the containers, you'll find basil growing in all types, from empty olive oil cans to window boxes to fancy ceramic pots. Basil's growability provides even the landless a means to enjoy the herb's decorative qualities, as well as its delicately perfumed fresh leaves.

Having success with potted basils is incredibly easy once a gardener composts a number of myths and misunderstandings that history has nurtured about containers. Pots and other vessels suitable for growing basil are made of the traditional clay and the more modern plastic. (We'll save whiskey barrels for later.) Clay is heavy and can break easily. Its porosity permits fast water loss, up to 80 percent more than plastic during winter. During the short days and low light levels of winter this attribute may help prevent overwatering. In summer, however, the ability of a pot to hold moisture is often advantageous. Plastic containers hold 30 percent more water than clay, an important consideration when root and foliage growth increase moisture requirements. (As plants mature, the disparity in water loss narrows to nil.)

Water loss also influences the temperature of the growing medium; the faster the loss, the lower the temperature. In a comparison of winter growth in clay and plastic pots, plants in plastic showed 15 percent more growth because soil temperatures varied as little as 1.8°F (1°C). When temperatures soar in summer, on the other hand, the more rapid cooling of clay pots become an advantage.

All containers used to grow basil plants should have good drainage. The best-draining pots are those with holes toward the center of the pot base; the number of holes is not as important as resting the pot on an open or porous surface (sand or gravel is great). One enduring gardening myth is that placing stones, broken clay, or other material in the bottom of a pot improves drainage; it actually does the opposite and causes the pot to hold more moisture.

If you choose plastic pots, keep in mind that color influences plant growth. Researchers discovered that light colored plastic pots permit roots to absorb light, causing plants to become stunted. Dark green pots protect plants from light and provide for normal growth.

Our choices for pots are divided. We like decorative clay pots for ornamental use when the splendor of a basil won't permit the heavy pruning necessary for the summer pesto race. For culinary plants, we like plastic pots in utilitarian green or black. Our workhorse basils are never going to win prizes at the county fair for beauty (health, maybe); these plants are going to be ravished regularly, and often, and their handsome looks are unlikely ever to be observed or flattered by an elegant container.

A row of five little basil plants looks really attractive freshly transplanted to an 18-inch (46-cm) window box, but in a short time they will be fighting each other for growing room and will become stunted from roots that are tangled, compressed, and stressed. Thus, if growth and yield are your yardsticks, the size of the container is central to success. In most instances, it will be necessary to repot any plant several times during the summer (see page 45). Growing multiple basil plants in a single large pot is difficult because crowding may cause disease problems. Multiple single pots provide better control over growth, air circulation, and nutrient levels. There's no reason you can't group your pots of basil to make them more attractive, if you're of such a mind.

Large wooden barrels have become summer favorites for herbs and flowers. With the large mass of growing medium required for such a container, some special techniques are helpful to assure bountiful harvests.

The first thing to keep in mind is that your basil plants aren't likely to need all the growing medium that the barrel will hold; 12 to 16 inches (30 to 40 cm) are probably sufficient for a typical summer of growth. The remainder of the container may be filled with broken cinder blocks, bricks, even that annoying Styrofoam dunnage from mail order packages.

With these super-large, outdoor containers, good drainage is as important as it is difficult to achieve. Days of rain can soak the large amount of medium, an especially dangerous condition for young transplants. If the container does not have several holes in the base, drill seven 3/4-inch (2 cm) diameter holes in the bottom, one in the middle and six in a circle 6 to 8 inches (15 to 20 cm) from the center. To further enhance drainage (and before adding the dampened growing

medium), put several inches of gravel under the barrel or raise it on bricks or cinder blocks. Siting the container where it receives full sun all day is important to
enhance the ability of nature to remove excess moisture and promote growth.

For barrels, instead of starting with transplants from 2.5-inch (6-cm) pots, start
with root-heavy plants from 6-inch (15-cm) containers; the larger plants will
have greater water transpiration capacity. Depending on the basil variety, space
plants 12 to 18 inches (30 to 46 cm) apart.

■ Repotting, watering, and feeding

When you hunger for basil, you don't want a container plant to slow its growth,
but that's what will happen if roots become densely wrapped around the outside
edge of the root ball. The signal for repotting basil is not the height or number of
leaves on a plant, but its root growth, and inspection of the roots is the only way
to ascertain whether a basil is pot-bound.

Forget what you've read about repotting into a container one size larger; the
rule-makers didn't have a brash, fast-growing, summer annual like basil in mind
when they wrote those regulations. Transplant seedlings growing in 2- to 2.5-inch
(5- to 6-cm) pots into 6-inch (15-cm) containers when they have at least three
pairs of leaves; in three to four summer weeks they'll probably be pot-bound and
ready to transplant into a big 12-inch (30-cm) container where they will probably spend the rest of their lives.

Does all this repotting seem to be a lot of trouble? Why not just stuff the little
seedling in a huge pot and keep it simple? The reason this shortcut method often
leads to trouble is basil's tendency to root rot. A big mass of wet growing medium
does not dry quickly enough to keep basil's air-seeking roots from suffocating.

Along with drainage holes and correctly-sized containers, the growing medium
that fills the pot plays an important role in basil success. Fast maturing crops like
basil do exceedingly well in containers filled with a soft, spongy, well-drained soilless growing medium. A wide array of these packaged container mixes are available at garden centers and hardware stores that sell horticultural supplies. These
mixes have good drainage, as well as water retention, an unusual combination
that explains why their manufacture is a proprietary concern. Garden soil is not
appropriate because it drains too poorly in the unnatural confines of a pot; it also
often contains weed seeds and harmful disease organisms.

When to water is the eternal question facing container gardeners. A good bit
of experience and artistry are involved in reading the signals that plant and pot

Transplant seedlings growing in 2- to 2½-inch (5- to 6-cm) pots into 6-inch (15 cm) containers when they have at least 3 pairs of leaves. This is a good time to prune to encourage branching.

provide. Many environmental factors govern the loss of water in a container: root structure, growing medium, pot type, and plant size. The goal is to water in such a way that the plant is fully irrigated but will dry quickly to prevent the roots from living in a soggy world. The gardener needs to remain flexible to the plant's needs to perform this task skillfully.

While many herbs can be left unwatered until they begin to show signs of stress, basil is not one. Here it is better to read the growing medium than the plant. Soilless mixes change color from dark to light as they dry: look before you water. The weight of the pot is another cue: heft before you water. Regularity in irrigating potted basils is a virtue to be honored, but don't be governed by a fixed schedule.

Basils are fast growing, heavy feeders and big yields are the result of steady growth and rich soil. Providing nutrients to a potted basil is essential, especially when soilless media are used. The nutrients in fertilizers may be inorganic or organic, but the key nutrient is nitrogen. A number of water-soluble packaged fertilizers are available; avoid those that are formulated for acid-loving plants. A good organic fertilizer is fish emulsion. Soilless growing media often lack not just the essential nutrients of nitrogen, phosphorous, and potassium, but micronutrients such as boron, copper, manganese, and molybdenum. Some fertilizers have been specially formulated with trace elements for plants grown in soilless media and it is prudent to use them, although not essential. A 20-10-20 (20 percent nitrogen, 10 percent phosphorus, 20 percent potassium) formula will produce excellent growth. Avoid fertilizers that obtain their nitrogen from ammonium; calcium nitrate sources are best. Always mix according to manufacturer's directions.

It is usually necessary to feed container basils once a week. As with watering, however, it is best to avoid date-based frequency schedules. A good rule of thumb is to fertilize mature basils every third or fourth irrigation.

If you'd rather avoid liquid fertilizers, pelletized nutrients are available. The pellets, actually plasticized membranes, are mixed with the growing medium during potting; when in contact with water, the pellets release nourishment slowly over a period of months and are quite satisfactory. An all-purpose 14-14-14 formula is commonly available and works well.

As summer fades, temperature swings and declining daylight produce slowed growth and increased threats from disease; under these conditions, one is tempted to bring big, summer-grown plants indoors. Avoid giving in to the temptation. The plants will be too big to gain enough sustenance from your fluorescent lights. But don't despair. There are alternatives for the gardener who craves fresh basil.

▪ An indoor basil garden

A few purists rumble against the use of food out of season, feeling that freshness is compromised when produce doesn't come from the back yard. This is more misplaced morality than it is home-grown passion; it's summer somewhere on earth every day—and summer can be surprisingly close to home.

With a little planning, winter's gloom need not mean an absence of fresh basil; instead the cold months can host an indoor herbal Eden. Fine, you say, for the owner of a greenhouse, but how do you make an Eden when big pots won't balance on narrow windowsills?

It is as easy to produce fresh basil in the basement or a spare closet as it is outdoors. The way to winter basil is to modify the techniques for growing seedling transplants and create an indoor garden under lights. At first this may seem difficult to do while obeying the basil axiom that many plants are better than one. Change the scale, we say, and grow basil in seedling flats under fluorescent lights, then harvest it *alla Genovese*.

To start your indoor basil garden, follow the earlier directions on starting seedlings under lights. Instead of twelve rows in the flat, use five to eight; this will

With a little planning, winter's gloom need not mean an absence of basil.

Irrigate and fertilize your tray of indoor-grown basil as if it contained seedlings.

provide extra growing room later on. Instead of transplanting the seedlings at the first true leaf stage (about two weeks from sowing), begin thinning them by yanking every other one, roots and all; take as many as you need for dinner. This process can go on for several weeks until the rows are thinned to one plant every half-inch (1 cm) or so; at this point the remaining seedlings will probably be at the four- to six-leaf stage and traditional harvesting using scissors can begin. (See Harvesting basil below.)

Continue to irrigate and fertilize the tray as if it contained seedlings. As your winter basil branches and grows taller, you may raise the light fixtures or leave them be. The leaves should not be damaged by growing right up into the fluorescent tubes. Continue cutting stems to harvest.

Root growth will probably slow after about four months. This is the time to start another tray of seedlings, but keep harvesting the first batch and maintain them by removing dead or discolored leaves and any withered or diseased plants. The plants will probably continue on for another month until they become too ragged and stop growing. Toss out the old flat and cultivate the new.

A basil garden under lights in a basement or a closet is a detour probably as far from Genoa as a basil lover's search for the perfect winter leaf can go, but with careful varietal selection, the plants grown at home should be as full of aromatic subtleties as any Ligurian would expect.

■ Harvesting basil

During their summer growth, basil plants are desperate to reproduce. Their flowers come quickly. Although home gardeners may not think of basil as a flowering plant, it is often grown for its blooms.

'African Blue', 'Anise', 'Cinnamon', 'Holly's Painted', and lemon basils have good appeal in arrangements. If stems are freshly cut and the water in the vase is changed every day, the basil spikes may keep for four weeks. Commercial growers appreciate basil flowers for their high essential oil content, machine-harvesting the plants in flower to capture oil for perfumes and food flavorings.

In the Grand Design of Nature, basil plants are supposed to sprout, grow, flower, set seed, and reproduce. That's the way to preserve the species, and it may help farmers and florists, but imitating Nature sure cuts down on the amount of pesto that can be made from a single plant. When stems flower, their foliage production ends.

Home gardeners have learned to frustrate basil's drive for flowers and keep it producing foliage all summer. By pruning plants before the flower heads form at stem tips, the plant is forced to grow more branches to meet Nature's goals.

Nature has programmed basil stems to produce a certain number of leaves before initiating a flower; the number varies among species and varieties. Nipping the flowers as they form does not stimulate new foliage; in fact, it actually encourages flowers to form in the axils of the leaves. To regenerate vegetative growth, basil stems must be cut deeply. It's almost never too soon to begin pruning culinary basils, and the moment of transplanting to the garden, when the seedling is at the six-leaf stage, is a good time to start. Basils from seed sown directly in the garden get the same treatment: start pruning at six to eight leaf pairs.

When harvesting foliage, do not pull leaves from the plant. Cut the stem with scissors or a sharp knife, removing enough of the stem to leave only 2 to 4 leaves.

When harvesting foliage, do not pull leaves from the plant; instead remove enough of the stem to leave only two to four leaves. Scissors or a sharp knife work best for harvesting. The stems should be cut cleanly so the wound heals quickly; it is difficult to do this with your fingernails on large-diameter branches. In as little as three weeks, the pruned stem will have regrown two to four new, harvestable branches. Managed in this way, several basil plants can be harvested alternatively through the summer to provide a steady supply of aromatic leaves.

Timing the harvest is easy. If you are going to use the basil immediately, pick it just before you need it. For long-term preservation, cut basil when the leaves are not wet. If you intend on drying basil, take it indoors or to a shady outdoor area for sorting and tying into bunches; do not dry basil in the sun. As you sort, remove any dirty, wilted, bug-eaten leaves, or any with dark spots. Brush any grit from the leaves. If the basil is so dirty you have to wash it, rinse the leaves quickly and pat dry, or place in front of a fan to help evaporate all moisture.

■ Keeping harvested basil fresh

The best way to keep basil fresh for a day or two is to re-cut the leafy stems and place them in a jar of water away from sunlight. Wetting the leaves, a practice sometimes suggested to retain freshness, tends to discolor the foliage. For longer shelf-life, cover the jar and the basil stems with a plastic bag and place it in the refrigerator; this method usually keeps the basil fresh for seven to ten days. Keep in mind, however, that temperatures inside refrigerators often vary and basil is cold-sensitive. While published research is not unanimous, there is agreement that temperatures below 45°F (7°C) can cause basil leaves to become discolored. A study by University of Michigan scientists indicates that basil has increased shelf-life when harvested after 6 p.m. and kept at temperatures between 50 and 68°F (10 and 20°C).

■ Drying basil

Two methods are traditionally used to dry basil. The simplest is to hang leafy stems to dry. Bundle three to five stems with string, twine, or rubber bands, then hang in a well-ventilated place away from direct sun.

The second method utilizes large screens for drying individual leaves. Fine mesh such as window screens or, even better, old screen doors can be used; otherwise make a frame from 1 by 2-inch (2.5 by 5-cm) lumber and staple screen to it. Place screens across sawhorses so that air circulates around and through the leaves. A drying shed, enclosed porch, or attic is usually a good location for setting up the screens, but any room can be used as long as it has good air circulation.

To prepare the basil for drying, remove the large leaves from the stems and lay them in a single layer on the screens; small leaves can be dried on their stems. Turn the leaves every three or four days. Basil will take from five to ten days or more to dry, depending on the humidity and temperature in the drying area.

Inspect the basil daily, especially in humid weather, removing any diseased leaves.

Dried basil leaves should crackle and crumble when rubbed between your fingers. If the leaves give or bend, they have not dried sufficiently. To remove the last bit of moisture, spread the leaves on baking sheets and place them in a very low oven, set at 150 to 200°F (65 to 93°C), for three to five minutes. The leaves should be crisp. Overdried leaves will become brown and bitter.

Whole leaves retain the finest flavor; crumbled leaves quickly lose their essential oils and pungency. Pack whole dried basil leaves in clean jars with tight lids. If the leaves have dried on their stems, carefully remove them. Label the jars and date them before storing in a cool, dark place. Dried basil has a shelf-life of about one year.

■ Freezing

Freezing basil is the least favorable way to preserve it. Most of the flavor disappears and the leaves turn dark. However, if you have an abundance of basil to preserve, these instructions provide the best freezer results.

Pack clean, dry basil leaves in pint (475 ml) plastic bags or airtight containers, label, and place in the freezer. If you want to pack the leaves in larger containers, first freeze the whole leaves individually on baking sheets, then transfer to the containers or freezer bags. This method of flash freezing separates the leaves so they don't lump together and may be extracted singly. Remove the leaves as you need them. Frozen leaves turn dark and mushy, so do not allow them to thaw. Add the frozen leaves to soup or sauce when you need them.

Basil freezes fairly well when chopped with a little oil. It still turns dark and its flavor fades, but it still has enough punch to brighten winter soups, sauces, and stews. You may also freeze pesto in half- or one-cup (120- or 240-ml) quantities in small plastic containers. Frozen pesto tastes best when the garlic is left out and added just before it is used. Extra cheese and olive oil will improve the taste of thawed pesto, while chopped fresh parsley increases the green color.

■ Getting the most from your plants

Responding with energetic abandon to the stimulus of hot sunny days and warm nights, basil grows as if it were a green, leafy vegetable rather than a hard-scrabble herb. This quick growth is reminiscent of a hungry teenager bent on emptying the refrigerator.

Unlike the typical teenager, basil is not seeking empty calories; this herb craves nitrogen to sustain its rapid growth. As we mentioned in the propagation section, nitrogen is easily supplied by fertilizer. Organic blood meal is high in nitrogen; calcium nitrate is the preferred inorganic form. (Tests at Purdue University showed that ammonium nitrate, the other common source of nitrogen, decreased plant height.)

All-purpose fertilizers containing nitrogen, phosphorus, and potassium should be applied to the garden bed prior to seeding or transplanting. Once plants are harvestable, apply fortnightly side-dressings of all-purpose liquid fertilizer high in nitrogen (or specialized nitrogen fertilizers such as granular calcium nitrate); this is commonly performed by scratching granular fertilizer into the top crust around the plants or by watering with liquid feed. Where the area to cover is too large for a watering can, use a hose attached to a siphon that pulls nutrient concentrate from a bucket and mixes it with water at a predetermined rate. Dry fertilizers should be watered after being applied. A good nutrient supply, plus intense light, are necessary to maintain dark color on purple basils.

Irrigation of basil may be necessary in many parts of the country to prevent the wilting that slows growth, damages roots, and stunts plants; one inch (2.5 cm) of water per week is sufficient in the absence of rain. (Special instructions for irrigating container grown plants are found above on page 46.)

When basil plants need nutrients or water, or have become diseased, they have already begun to lose valuable growing time. First-time gardeners need to understand BasilTalk. Learning this visual basil language is uncomplicated and the vocabulary is small.

One of the first words of BasilTalk humans learn is the call for water—this the plant does by wilting. If the basil's ground is dry, water it quickly. However, if the soil is wet, and it's still wilting, the plant may have root rot from too much water or disease. Leaf shedding often accompanies root and vascular diseases (see page 53).

Leaf color is also an important indicator of plant health. Light green or yellowish leaves on a normally dark-leafed plant indicate a lack of nitrogen. A quick watering with a liquid fertilizer usually remedies the deficit. Purple-leaved basils often show their lack of nitrogen with lighter-colored leaves. Green or variegated green and purple leaves on 'Dark Opal', 'Purple Ruffles', and 'Rubin' are usually associated with genetic weakness caused by breeding.

Other discoloration of the leaves identify phosphorus and potassium deficiencies. If the underside of green leaf stems, or petioles, turn purple and the discoloration spreads to the leaf's main veins, phosphorus deficiency is probably to blame. Yellow leaf margins signal a lack of potassium.

Holes in the leaves often bespeak insects; Japanese beetles, slugs, and grasshoppers are basil lovers, too. Japanese beetles and grasshoppers are best controlled through ground treatment that kills the immature insects developing underground. Relief from adult pests may be obtained by covering plants during the day with breathable garden fabric that allows light, air, and water to pass through.

Slugs live in dark, moist places: rocks, sidewalks, fence posts, foundations, even heavy mulches. Slugs have an abiding affinity for basil. The traditional lid of beer, while it may catch and drown many slugs, is a rather ineffective method of control. A more fool-proof method is a 5-inch (13-cm) high copper fence around the basil patch; copper reacts to slugs' soft bodies by creating a nonlethal electrical charge. Long-lasting copper is easy to cut and bend, but it is expensive. Building-supply companies often stock rolls of copper for flashing on roofs. When sowing seeds in the garden, it's wise to install the copper before the seedlings germinate.

Copper fence is an effective way to control slugs.

■ Diseases

Although basil is a tough, vigorous, easily grown annual that is relatively disease free, it would be foolish to pretend that it is not susceptible to some environmental challenges.

Careful attention to sanitation and moisture control are simple measures that can lessen disease problems on basil and many other herbs. Plant debris can harbor many diseases and should be cleared away from the garden on a regular basis. Growing containers should not be reused unless they have been soaked in a detergent-bleach combination and thoroughly scrubbed.

Moisture-born diseases can be controlled in several ways. Proper siting and spacing permits drying air to flow through and around plants. Space should always be left between plants and fences, foundations, or other dense structures to facilitate air movement.

On occasion, basil seedlings will succumb to *Pythium* and *Rhizoctonia*, two soil diseases that cause sudden wilting or collapse of the tender seedling stems. *Pythium* does its work on young roots in wet soil, while *Rhizoctonia* strikes when soil is moderately moist, attacking the stem, usually where it meets the soil, and causing it to rot. These two diseases are controlled by sowing seed in a sterile medium such as vermiculite or a disease-free soilless mix. While soil-borne, they may also travel on moisture. *Pythium* moves in the moisture; *Rhizoctonia* is often spread by splashing water. Keeping seedlings as dry as possible provides partial control of both diseases.

Moisture also plays an important role in the spread of diseases that attack adult basils, particularly those in which leaves drop prematurely or produce dark streaks on stems; both symptoms indicate basil shoot blight, a generic term for two diseases with similar outward expressions. *Erwinia*, a bacterial disease, is a serious problem for greenhouse growers, especially those growing basil during the winter in cold climates. It's also a problem for summer gardeners. In addition to premature leaf drop and dark stem lesions, *Erwinia* causes leaf spotting. The disease is particularly troublesome in hot, humid climates. It is often found in plant debris and on leaves; splashing water may spread it. Seeds harvested from infected plants sometimes carry the bacteria. Stem damage and harvesting provide common ways for *Erwinia* to enter a plant. Fingers that touch an infected plant may carry the disease to other basils.

Prevention is the chief method for controlling *Erwinia*. Spacing to permit air to dry the leaves and plant interior is one avenue. Watering without wetting leaves is also beneficial. Sprays such as Top Cop and Bordeaux mixture, used by some organic growers, may provide protection. In experiments at North Carolina State University, Jeanine Davis found that bark mulches reduced the incidence of shoot blight on basil. However, mulched plants produced somewhat reduced yields.

Another disease with symptoms somewhat similar to *Erwinia* is *Fusarium*, a disabling wilt disease with long-term soil persistence that has only recently appeared in the United States. This is not the *Fusarium* that causes tomato plants to wilt unexpectedly but is a close relative specific to basil; scientists have named it *Fusarium oxysporum* f. sp. *basilicum*. Although it first appeared in the former Soviet Union in 1956, its spread has been halting. It turned up in Italy in 1975 and France in 1982. It appeared in the U.S. in 1992 and was identified by Robert L. Wick of the University of Massachusetts on basil plants grown hydroponically.

Fusarium fungi live in the soil and invade susceptible host plants through their roots; from there, they move into a plant's stems, blocking the vascular system and causing the plant to wilt and die. The disease can be transmitted by infected soil, infected plants, and contaminated seeds. The fungi may live in the soil for many years in a dormant state (this inactive condition is sometimes referred to as the "resting spores" stage) and become rambunctious when their specific host plant is grown nearby.

Keeping contaminated seed from U.S. fields and gardens has been the first defensive tactic against *Fusarium*. Many seed merchants have begun testing their imported basil seeds to make sure what they sell is untainted. An experimental hot water bath has been shown to kill the disease on seeds, but the temperature at which it dies is very close to the degree at which the seed is killed, making the bath difficult to use without heat-sensing equipment.

Anthony P. Keinath of Clemson University has suggested several ways to beat the disease. He points out that *Fusarium* has been controlled in tomato and chrysanthemum crops by raising soil pH to as high as 7.5 and fertilizing with nitrate nitrogen. In the former Soviet Georgia, methyl bromide has been used successfully to treat infested soil, and in India researchers have mixed the fungus *Trichoderma* into the soil to reduce *Fusarium* wilt and increase basil growth.

Home gardeners have little to fear from this *Fusarium* because it attacks only basil. In the unlikely event that soil becomes infested with the fungus, future basil crops could be produced in pots with an uncontaminated growing medium.

▪ Harvesting and storing basil seeds

Basil seeds are not expensive, so the desire to save money by producing your own seeds is rarely driven by cost. There is a time in every basil lover's life, however, when a special variety is so captivating that it becomes indispensable. Although the plant's seed may have come from a catalog, it may also have been presented by a friend whose memory or gift you particularly cherish. So this could be the time, and the basil, that triggers your desire to begin a part of home gardening that is rarely indulged anymore—seed production.

Half a century ago, relatively few gardeners grew basil, but those who did often found the easiest way to make sure they had seed for next year's crop was to save it from their own plants. Growing seed to keep a favorite plant going may become a necessity in a quick-changing world where fickle seed merchants jump to the newest variety and abandon the old reliables. (The Redwood City Seed Company noted on its 25th anniversary in 1996 that half the seeds offered in its first catalog were no longer available.)

Basil is one of the most prolific herbs and one of the easiest from which to save seed. A single flower stem may contain 120 to 240 seeds, or nutlets, all of them living embryos ready to become the next generation of basils.

For the home gardener without much space, the most difficult task in seed production is keeping the seed true to its parent. Basils are self-fertile, and a single plant will produce seeds by itself; problems arise if pollen from another species or cultivated variety finds its way (often through the interest of a bee) to the flowers on the plant you are using to grow seed. When two basils cross, only a small number of seeds remain true to the parent and a great many have characteristics of both plants. With proper pruning, basils can be kept from flowering, so it is possible, by permitting only one plant to flower, to have a high degree of certainty that a cross has not occurred (providing other basils are not flowering in nearby gardens).

The seed-growing process may take three months or more from the time of sowing, depending on variety. The best way to approach seed growing is to set aside a plant or plants which will be used only for seed collection. Harvest other plants for their foliage.

If you have several varieties of basil from which you want to save seed, there are a number of ways to keep them from hybridizing. The simplest is to stagger collection over several years. Seed remains viable for three to five years with little special care and enough seed for several seasons can be collected on rotation.

An alternative to staggered-year harvests is protecting selected plants from pollinators. Screen-wire cages placed over plants prevent all but the tiniest pollen-seeking insects from causing unintended crosses. Cages are much better than spunbonded plastic garden fabric, which lowers light levels and traps moisture around plants. Trapped moisture causes diseases, especially basil shoot blight.

Seed collection is influenced by basils' flowering characteristics. All the blossoms on a basil inflorescence do not open at the same time; they start blooming at the base of the spike and open upward in a process that may take a week or two. After the central terminal has begun flowering, side shoots pop out and eventually flower, too. This process means that a single plant will have seeds in a variety of states at any given time.

After all the flowers on a single spike have bloomed and the petals are gone or removed, it is easy to see the small seeds. Light tan, they begin to darken as they ripen. Once all the seeds are ripe, from the bottom to the top of the spike, it is time to snip it off and place it in a paper bag where the second process of moisture loss begins. Write the name of the basil and date of harvest on the bag. You

After all the flowers on a single spike have bloomed and the petals are gone or removed, it is easy to see the small seeds.

Once all the seeds on a spike are ripe, snip it off and place it in a paper bag where the second process of moisture loss begins.

should cut the stems in the afternoon of a sunny, hot day when the seed heads are dry. This timing will reduce the chances of disease ruining the seeds as they dry, or worse, having the seeds carry the disease into the next season.

One of the great joys of January, the darkest month of the winter, is cleaning basil seeds. The aroma wafting up from the dried stems fills the room immediately and releases wonderful memories. The promise of spring fills the air.

Seeds are cleaned on wire screens that vary in mesh size; the top screen has the widest mesh. The process is designed to separate chaff from the seed as it falls through each level of a screen pyramid. Screens are usually 12-inch-square (30-cm-sq.) frames made from smooth hardwood that is 3/4-inch (2-cm) thick by 1½ inches (4 cm) deep. The screen is attached to the bottom of the frame and a wooden bead is placed over the screen edge so that the ragged edges do not catch and tear hands or clothing. A few seed merchants sell the finished screens. To clean basil seed, the top screen should be 1/8-inch (3-mm) mesh, the middle screen 1/12-inch (2-mm) mesh, and the bottom screen 1/20-inch (1-mm) mesh.

Seeds are cleaned on a tower of three wire screens.

Once you've piled the seed heads on the top screen, rub the dry plant material to separate the seed. Continue until the top screen is bare.

Remove the top screen and lightly rub the plant material; lingering seeds will fall through the mesh while most of the chaff remains on the middle screen.

Make a tower of these three screens on top of a newspaper when you are ready to start seed cleaning. Although it isn't required, the work goes smoother and is kinder to your hands if stems are first removed from the seed heads. The seed heads come clean if you hold the base of the stem with one hand and slip it up through your other hand.

Once you've piled the seed heads on the top screen, rub the dry plant material to separate the seed. When you are satisfied that all seed is dislodged and has fallen through, remove the top screen and lightly rub the plant material; lingering seeds will fall through the mesh while most of the chaff remains on the middle screen. Remove the middle screen.

The bottom screen now contains seeds and small pieces of chaff. A gentle breeze from a fan, or your mouth, blown across the top of the screen will remove most of the chaff. Tipping the screen and gently shaking the seeds will make it easier to blow the chaff away. Use a stiff card to scoop up the seeds and place them in paper packets or envelopes labeled with the name and harvest date.

Basil seed can remain viable for three to five years sitting in a cupboard, but this method of storage is risky. High temperatures and moisture drain vigor from seed and decrease its germination. Proper seed storage limits these environmen-

Remove the middle screen. The bottom screen now contains seeds and small pieces of chaff. Remove the chaff with a gentle breeze across the top of the screen.

Use a stiff card to scoop up the seeds and place them in paper packets or envelopes labeled with the name and harvest date.

tal hazards. Many merchants now use airtight foil packs to protect seed. Once you open them to remove some seed, fold the cut top over twice to seal it. For lengthy storage, foil or paper packets may be placed in zip-lock bags from which as much air as possible has been expressed; the bags are then kept in a refrigerator or freezer. Author Helen Darrah wrote that she had grown "fine plants" from basil seed frozen for fifteen years.

Growing basil and saving its seed is another step in the process that provides gardeners with knowledge and understanding of the plants they grow. The process may give you a sense of pride and mastery, but it is well to remember that most of the work was accomplished by a simple plant which you only tended and observed. What may be more important is the poetic side of this process. Growing ancient plants such as basil is a great way to stay connected to the past, sharing in that beautiful mystery that filled Virgil and Pliny with wonder centuries ago.

The Individualistic World of Basils
varieties and how they grow

If the definition of poetry allowed that it could be composed

with the products of the field as well as with words,

pesto would be in every anthology.

—MARCELLA HAZAN, *The Classic Italian Cook Book*

To those smitten with basil, it is hard to contain the urge to seek new and unusual forms of the herb. Breeders and seed merchants are just as eager to tempt us annually with astonishing varieties from all over the world. The synergy created in the marketplace by these two forces has turned the modern basil garden into a multicolored blaze of beauty and aroma, a reflection of the herb's strong allure and gardeners' insistent fascination with the novel and the peculiar.

While many basils offered today seem fresh and wondrous, they are actually old hat in their native habitat, ubiquitous as weeds, with centuries of use for flavor and medicine. Others, the spawn of breeders, full of flash and bemedaled, have less familiar antecedents.

The 1930s, already old enough to be dowdy in memory, was a decade when nothing was new and times were hard. Yet basil devotees from that era remember being excited by a small-leaved dwarf, purple basil. During the 1940s, Gertrude Foster and her husband Philip kept that purple basil, a lemon from Thailand, and many other heirloom herbs at their Laurel Hill Herb Farm. The purple basil seeds were still around in the 1962 catalog of Plantation Gardens in Rustburg, Virginia. Bruce and Eleanor Chalfin of Plantation Gardens also offered three other purple basil varieties: a large, curly type; another dwarf; and a sweet or common. Their list of green-leaved basils included seven varieties, one imported from Vilmorin in

France. A 1967 seed list from Jim and Madalene Hill of Hilltop Herb Farm in Cleveland, Texas, contained many of the same basils, including the dwarf purple variety.

Basils were different then. "Back in those days," Madalene Hill recalled, "sweet basil had purple spots on its leaves." 'Those days' were also a time of discovery, when strangers showed up with new basils in their hands. As a result of two such encounters, Hill brought a cinnamon basil and a basil with a reddish-purple ball head into the United States seed trade from Mexico. Park Seed Company sold the ball-headed basil for years, but no longer catalogs it; the cinnamon remains available.

The spirit of collecting the new and preserving the old that animated the Fosters, the Chalfins, the Hills, and many other American herb pioneers is still with us. Succeeding generations of herb growers have carried on their work, adding to the old germ plasm, or trying to recreate it where the original has disappeared.

Cyrus Hyde, the herb collector, nurseryman, and breeder, became frustrated over his inability to find the small-leaved dwarf purple basil about which Mrs. Foster had written. In the early 1970s, he set out to create a new one. After considerable breeding work, Hyde had a basil similar to Foster's that he called 'Well-Sweep Miniature Purple'.

Not every grower has to work so hard for the new. In the spring of 1983, Peter Borchard of Companion Plants bent over and saw something curious sprouting in a garden bed of his nursery. It was a new hybrid purple-leaved basil that he called 'African Blue', a presumed cross of an African camphor basil and 'Dark Opal'.

The interest in preserving plants from the past inspires tenacity and dedication. For thirty years Janet Burns cultivated a lemon-scented basil in Carlsbad, New Mexico. Her perseverance has been rewarded by Native Seeds Search who introduced her basil as 'Mrs. Burns' Lemon'.

Few basil growers have the opportunity to see the hometowns of their plants. Conrad Richter, of the well-known Canadian firm Richters, has been making seed pilgrimages to exotic spots for years. On a trip to the Volta region of Ghana in 1994, he saw many different basils. "While the locals know the basils, and occasionally use them for food and medicine," he recalls, "they only make distinctions at the species level, assigning local names to each."

Richter's excursion into Africa was memorable for another reason: he came down with malaria. "Silly man that I am," he says, "I would happily risk malaria again to collect more basils in Ghana." At the vanguard of seedsmen who encourage local people to grow native plants for seeds, Richters now maintains seed growing and collection projects in Ghana, Mexico, Nepal, and India.

Sometimes a single individual collects and helps to introduce little-known basils. Nearly twenty years ago, Richard Dufresne got Park Seed excited about four basils—lemon, cinnamon, anise, and spice—that the company continues to offer to this day. Another passionate basil collector, Helen Darrah, offered samples of her seeds to W. Atlee Burpee. Fascinated by basil's genetic variability, Burpee's long-time breeder Ted Torrey used Darrah's seed to create two new basils, 'Green Ruffles' and 'Purple Ruffles'. Today, younger breeders such as James E. Simon and his assistant Mario Morales are busy fashioning dramatic new basils from seeds collected around the world. Their work at Purdue University is motivated by the desire to create basils that are ornamental as well as useful and fragrant.

Collectors and breeders have long maintained an uneasy relationship. Breeders often rely on seeds from collector-hobbyists. Collectors often worry that new seeds will push old favorites into obscurity. Despite these differences, collectors and breeders are joined in spirit; the chief tool that shapes their horticultural passions is chance, nature's creative principle. To deal with unpredictability in their work, both collectors and breeders need to develop a clever eye for variation and an instinct for both the possibilities and the limits of plants. With their voracious hunger for the new and the old, gardeners owe past and present basil collectors and breeders a large debt.

■ Our basils, our methods

When we began our basil project, we didn't intend to grow every basil variety available, just a goodly representation of what is sold in the United States. We ordered basil plants and seeds, just as any gardener might. We wanted to see what was available in this country and we wanted to purchase the widest possible variety.

We also cajoled friends and strangers to bring us basil seeds. A well-traveled herb lover showed up one day with a packet of seeds purchased on a trip to Thailand. In addition to a lot of foreign writing, the packet bore two words in English: holy basil. The drawing on the envelope resembled holy basil, a positive sign. And, in fact, the tiny, brown seeds inside the packet produced *Ocimum tenuflorium*, Indian holy basil, the only seed we sowed (of the half dozen making the claim) that actually produced the real thing.

We conducted our project during the summer of 1995. At that time, a number of basils were not yet in commerce (some were not ready for release by breeders or the seeds were still held in private collections). Regarding it unfair to tempt readers with as-yet-unavailable basils, we have eliminated these plants from the purview of this book.

We grew 4,000 plants for our trials; these included nearly 100 basils, some duplicates from different sources to check seed quality and identity. We tried to grow and keep thirty-two plants of each basil purchased, an often difficult task because of disease problems, some of which may have come with the seeds. After looking at the basils and sniffing them assiduously, we were convinced that at least one-third were traveling under assumed names or were duplicates; one wasn't even a basil.

Both of us needed plants for our own purposes. Susan took three or four of each variety to her Maryland garden. She sat with the plants in the garden to divine their aroma and taste as most gardeners do, by rubbing and sniffing leaves, then chewing them to express their taste. Then she used the leaves in her kitchen. Over in Virginia, Tom's greenhouse bulged with basils. Those in six-inch (15-cm) containers were used for observation and photography. Larger pots indoors and out were kept to fill in for failures and to determine suitability for container culture.

Having immersed ourselves in basil for a number of happy, hot, sunny months, we want to issue several caveats to reassert what horticulturists have known for centuries. Although we list a number of horticultural characteristics for each basil grown, even plants that share the same seed packet can look dissimilar when grown side by side. We are reporting data as we found it; some variations are inevitable. That's caveat number one.

We started our basils under basement lights in mid to late May, a season that can be quite hot in our area of the east coast. The seedlings were transplanted during early June when temperatures can be breathtaking. Many of the plants continued to grow outdoors until October when the space was needed for other plants. Here's our second caveat: heat and other environmental conditions have ways of altering plant growth, enlarging it or speeding it up. Leaf size and color are subject to similar alterations for the same reasons. When we say that our purple Thai basil, for instance, was garden ready thirty days after sowing, it is important to consider the conditions that led to that conclusion. Had we sown the purple Thai earlier in the season, cooler temperatures might have meant another week to produce the same plant. What we hope you'll get from using our information, besides gloriously healthy plants, are relationships and landmarks that will help you understand basils and how to grow them. Any basil's growth depends on soil fertility, wind velocity, the number of hours of sun, and innumerable other factors. Use our numbers as guides, not as orthodoxy.

Several pieces of our information may need explanation to clarify their usefulness. Knowing how quickly a basil flowers gives gardeners notice of harvest time; it also tells them how soon to prune to prevent flowering. The date from sowing to first flowering makes sense for seed-grown plants only. Plants from cuttings are produced from terminal tips and may have unseen buds that will produce flowers quickly. We usually prune rooted cutting tips when they are transplanted to prevent premature flower emergence and to start the new plant branching quickly. The number of leaves on a stem at flowering is another way to time harvests; it also provides a clue to how many branches to expect from an unpinched main stem (once the central stem ceases flowering, a branch will rise from the joint where leaf meets stem). Because flowering ends upward growth for the stem, heights and widths at flowering provide hints to the final height and width of unpruned plants. Width and height may increase after initial flowering by 15 to 25 percent because of new branch growth.

Many of the basils we grew during the summer of 1995 were exciting and mysterious. They were beautiful to see and fun to grow but their plain names hid their charms; they had "we've-got-to-call-it-something" monikers like 'New Guinea', 'Thai', 'Cuban', 'Puerto Rican', and 'Green'.

In many cases we wish basil names were more descriptive. Whether the naming process is tightly controlled or casual, a plant's name defines it, explains who it is and maybe how it differs from others of its ilk. Basil's familiar names can be misplaced, inaccurate, even false, but they often become tightly attached to the plant.

Botanists study plants with a nervous accuracy that puzzles many American gardeners. Taxonomy requires details that gardeners often overlook or can't see readily. We encountered many plants with different names that looked alike. We also grew plants that our seed sources could not identify botanically. In these cases, we thought it best to seek professional aid. Two respected plant scientists— James E. Simon of Purdue University and Arthur O. Tucker of Delaware State University —unraveled many mysteries of our basils' botany and chemistry. A few botanical identifications were impossible because no flowers, critical for any plant identification, could be had for study.

Dr. Tucker provided us with a list of tentative botanical names for the plants we grew. These names may be unfamiliar and difficult, but they are important for delineating intricate differences between plants. To our surprise, we ended up with many hybrid basils, probably the result of careless seed-growing techniques or crosses occuring naturally in native habitats. Most basil seed is produced in open fields; if differing species are grown too close to each other, hybridization may occur. When atypical plants are not rogued from the seed-growing area, additional hybridization may take place. Where Dr. Tucker has identified hybrids, the putative parentage is shown in parentheses beside the botanical name.

Chemical analysis of our basils' essential oils revealed the differences that our eyes and noses missed. While chemistry may at first appear out-of-place in a garden book, it is chemicals that make basils taste good. Basil's flavors and fragrances are so essential to its charm and usage that we would be remiss in not discussing their chemical basis. Chemistry is often what separates two basils that look alike; it's what makes one sweet basil tastier than another.

We've tried to give you a handle on taste and scent with the individual basil descriptions in this chapter. Susan has courageously put her sensitivity and knowledge on display for flavor and fragrance interpretation. We have also noted the primary chemicals in the essential oils of each basil. The way that nature has manipulated the chemicals in each variety's essential oils determines flavor and fragrance.

Few of us can identify single constituents of a plant's essential oils by smelling a leaf or chewing it. We tend to use food scents and tastes as markers. We talk about anise by referring to licorice, but what we are actually smelling is methyl chavicol. The soft, complex clove-laced aroma from the tiny leaves of the Italian basil 'Piccolo verde fino' is due to the predomination of flowery linalool and clove-scented eugenol in the plant's essential oils.

Bush basil is also high in linalool, but eugenol and a third chemical, the spicy, camphor-like 1,8-cineole, alter the essential oils significantly. Anise basil's overpowering scent derives from the anise-scented methyl chavicol and flowery linalool that make up nearly 80 percent of the essential oil of this aromatic class of basils.

The chemicals that give lemon basil its scent are the lemony citral (geraniol and neral) and linalool. The strong, distinctive clove aroma of 'Spice' basil (often mistakenly called 'Holy' basil) comes from the clove-scented eugenol and the anise-scented methyl chavicol. The distinctive aroma of cinnamon basil comes from cinnamon-scented methyl cinnamate. This chemistry is specific and constitutes one of the ways that you may know your basils.

Mario Morales, the Purdue research scientist who put together the chemical analysis of our plants, offers a couple of cautions. Genetic variations are common in seed-grown plants and the essential oils of individual plants may vary widely. Normally, scientists test the essential oils of thirty to sixty seed-grown plants of the same name; this large population gives them a better idea of the average essential oil chemistry and its variations. We didn't have enough plants to provide Dr. Morales with a definitive sample, but we were less interested in specific chemical values than we were in footnoting the key flavoring agents, something his tests did reveal.

Chemistry may be an arcane way to approach the flavor of America's favorite herb. Most people identify basil the way Susan does, by sniffing and chewing. The sensations that follow pleasurable olfactory incidents are deeply personal, unlike the chemical menu, because each individual reacts differently to the aroma and flavor of foods and their ingredients.

While the sense of smell has an almost limitless palate, taste buds perceive four basic sensations: salty, sour, sweet, and bitter. Taken separately, the nose may discern characteristics not perceived by the mouth. Though a basil may have a weak mint scent, its mint flavor may be forceful. A basil with a sweet aroma may have a bitter taste. To take account of these differences, we separate the aromas of each basil from its flavors. You must also remember that the separate sensory functions of smell and taste work together when we eat.

The fragrance and taste of most basils contain anise, mint, the spice of cinnamon and/or cloves, and floral tones. In our descriptions, we use anise to describe the sweet, green, herb-like scent or flavor similar to fennel. We use licorice when the anise-like aroma or taste is more intense, almost candy-sweet. The flavor of spearmint is common enough to be generic; we use peppermint when the mint is strong, peppery, or pungent. Orange mint describes the tea-like quality of the bergamot orange from which Earl Grey tea is derived. Then there are the spice notes. Sometimes "spice" denotes a cinnamon and clove combination, sometimes it indicates a subtler blend incorporating allspice, mace, ginger, or even cardamom. Floral tones vary from sweet grass and hyacinth to citrus. "Citrus" may refer to the flowery essence of lemon or orange blossoms, the aroma or taste of the fruit's juice, or even the oil or zest, which is heavier than either flower or fruit fragrances.

Some basils, particularly those with purple leaves, have a peculiar, dusky sensory trait that masks or obscures their fragrance and flavor. The result is a restrained sensory experience in which the palate and the nose are denied the clean, bright character of green-leaved basils.

A few terms apply to only a handful of basils. Some varieties taste slightly to very bitter, unpleasant to acrid. *Hotness* or *pungency* designates a sharp or penetrating quality in either odor or taste. These characteristics may derive from bitterness or a concentration of flavors; they may produce a strong odor or a burning sensation on the tongue. *Spicy* doesn't refer to hot, but to the presence of spices, most often a combination of cloves and cinnamon. *Musk* indicates a penetrating, persistent odor. *Resinous* pertains to the character of a natural resin like pine sap, or even turpentine.

One final caveat: most of the time basil is only a flavoring agent in the food we eat, modified by other ingredients. What matters is the way that basil acts in a dish. Your taste determines what kind of basil to use as well as how much.

The *Ocimum* genus is like a huge extended family, filled with doting parents, favorite aunts and uncles, kind grandparents, even the occasional oddball cousin. When we reflect on all the basils that we grew in the summer of 1995, we're amazed at the unexpected scents, shapes, and colors we encountered. After growing, tasting, and enjoying all these plants, we are certain of one thing: there is a basil here for everyone.

CLOCKWISE FROM UPPER LEFT: 'Dark Opal', 'Maenglak Thai Lemon', 'Lemon', 'Spicy Globe', and 'Green'.

■ A directory of basils

AFRICAN BLUE. *Ocimum* 'African Blue' (*Ocimum* 'Dark Opal' × *O. kilimandscharicum*.) The genesis of 'African Blue' basil is somewhat uncertain. Peter Borchard of Companion Plants in Athens, Ohio, discovered the hybrid growing in one of his seed beds in 1983. He believes it is a natural cross between *Ocimum* 'Dark Opal' and *O. kilimandscharicum*. The two basils had grown in adjoining beds in his seed production area.

'African Blue' basil is a large, bushy, energetic plant that produces blossom-fat, 6-inch (15-cm), purple-blushed flower spikes with large lavender blossoms. Typical leaves are 2¼ inches (6 cm) long by 1¾ inches (4.5 cm) wide, egg-shaped and pointed with a moderately serrated edge; the center of new leaves is often heavily brushed with purple which fades in time to a deep, bright green on top with deep purple veining; the leaf underside is more heavily colored with a reddish purple; stems are lightly hairy and suffused with violet. Plants grow 3 feet (91 cm) high or more in a season and as wide; their continuous growth and flower production creates an aura of unguarded splendor in the garden. Not a major culinary basil, but an excellent ornamental and a favorite for flower arrangements. When water in the vase is changed regularly, this basil will bloom and look good for three to four weeks.

REPRODUCED BY ROOTING STEM CUTTINGS.
HEIGHT AT FIRST FLOWERING: *2 feet (61 cm).*
PAIRS OF LEAVES ON FLOWERING STEM: *6.*
WIDTH AT FIRST FLOWERING: *25 inches (63 cm).*
AROMA AND TASTE: *Although the leaves have a typical mild basil-like aroma, the flavor is herby and has a strong balsam tendency with a hint of turpentine, not desirable qualities of a culinary plant. The scent derives from the flowery linalool and two camphor-based chemicals, 1,8-cineole and camphor.*

ANISE. *Ocimum basilicum* 'Anise'. There are a number of green-leaved, anise-scented basils available in the United States. They are called "anise" or "licorice", and "Thai". We are including most of them under this heading because of their similarities in appearance and aroma. We found significant differences in two Thai basils and they are listed under the headings "Purple Thai" and "True Thai".

The oldest of the anise basils sold by a major seed company is probably that offered by Park. A little less than two decades ago, Richard Dufresne brought the company a group of "flavored" basils, among them an anise-scented specimen from Iran. The seed had come from Kim Kuebel who, even as a college student was an avid herb collector. According to Dufresne, Kueble had obtained seed for the plant from a classmate who was from Iran. Park sells the seed under the name "Licorice Basil".

Heart-shaped leaves are dark green, varying in size by age but averaging 3 inches (7.5 cm) long by 1½ inches (4 cm) wide. The leaves are strongly veined; margins are noticeably serrated. Calyxes, bracts, and stems are green with a reddish-purple blush. Medium-sized light pink flowers are carried in whorls on 3- to 6-inch (8- to 15-cm) long inflorescences.

NORMALLY REPRODUCED FROM SEED.

TIMING: *At 70°F (21°C), germination is 3 days; transplant 13 days after sowing; garden ready 25 days after sowing.*

FIRST FLOWERING: *66 days from sowing.*

HEIGHT AT FIRST FLOWERING: *30 inches (76 cm).*

PAIRS OF LEAVES ON FLOWERING STEM: *8.*

WIDTH AT FIRST FLOWERING: *17 inches (43 cm).*

AROMA AND TASTE: *Slight differences in scent and flavor were detected. Leaves offer a spicy anise aroma with hints of mint and citrus. The best tasting clone came from Park and was rich with licorice followed by a warm spicy-mint flavor and finishing with cloves and cinnamon. Up to half the essential oil is the anise-flavored methyl chavicol. The generous amount of the flowery linalool in these clones was missing in the other Thai basils included in our list.*

BUSH GREEN.
Ocimum 'Bush Green'. Generic bush basils and named clones abound, although none appear to be the plant referred to as 'Minimum' as late as the 1960s. Aside from 'Bush Green', we found similar plants under the following names: 'Dwarf Bush', 'Dwarf Bush Fine Leaf', and 'Green Globe'.

Flowers on the Bush Green group of plants are white, appearing on branched inflorescences that make inverted pyramids. The flower heads hide in the foliage as they begin flowering but soon rise above it. Plants may be rather flat on top. Small, elongated green leaves are moderately veined with toothed margins. Stems appear smooth. Leaves are 5/8 to 1 inch (1.5 to 2.5 cm) long and 3/8 to 5/8 inch (1 to 1.5 cm) wide. The dense foliage on these formally shaped plants is handsome and fragrant, making them delightful ornamentals; in humid climates the foliage density can foster disease.

NORMALLY REPRODUCED FROM SEED.

TIMING: *At 70°F (21°C), germination is 3 days; transplant 13 days after sowing; garden ready 25 days after sowing.*

FIRST FLOWERING: *70 days from sowing.*

HEIGHT AT FIRST FLOWERING: *11 inches (28 cm).*

PAIRS OF LEAVES ON FLOWERING STEM: *8.*

WIDTH AT FIRST FLOWERING: *12 inches (30 cm).*

AROMA AND TASTE: *These small plants have a good basil perfume, predominantly of clove, cinnamon, and anise with a note of muskiness. The taste, on the other hand, is not strong and is green and minty with a trace of anise. The scent derives from a combination of the flowery-scented linalool, the spicy-camphorous 1,8-cineole, and spicy β-caryophyllene.*

CAMPHOR.
Ocimum kilimandscharicum. Named after Mount Kilimanjaro in Tanzania, *O. kilimandscharicum* retains something of its namesake—height. It is one of the tallest basils we grew, reaching nearly 3 feet (91 cm). Cyrus Hyde of Well-Sweep Herb Farm, our plant's source, says his cutting stock originated with the late Nancy Howard, a prominent member of the Herb Society of America who was responsible for adding a number of unusual herbs to the American inventory.

Camphor basils are known for their long, showy inflorescences which may reach 7 to 9 inches (18 to 23 cm), although they begin blooming at 4 to 5 inches (10 to 13 cm). The flower stems are fuzzy and filled with hairy, white buds that burst open into medium-sized white floral trumpets. The tan branches are strong, straight and woody, bearing dark green, strongly veined, pointed leaves that are 1½ to 3 inches (4 to 7.5 cm) long and 1 to 1¾ inches (2.5 to 4.5 cm) wide; leaf-margins are modestly scalloped.

NORMALLY REPRODUCED FROM SEED AND CUTTINGS.

TIMING: *At 70°F (21°C), germination is 3 days; transplant 15 days after sowing; garden ready 32 days after sowing.*

FIRST FLOWERING: *60 days from sowing.*

HEIGHT AT FIRST FLOWERING: *21 to 30 inches (53 to 76 cm).*

PAIRS OF LEAVES ON FLOWERING STEM: *7 to 10.*

WIDTH AT FIRST FLOWERING: *17 inches (43 cm).*

AROMA AND TASTE: *Camphorous, minty, musky, and inedible. A good ornamental for a spot where a fast-growing annual with height is needed. More than three-quarters of the essential oil is camphor and the spicy-camphorous 1,8-cineole.*

CINNAMON.

Ocimum basilicum 'Cinnamon'. The day Madalene Hill first saw this spicy Mexican basil was July 20, 1969, and the *Eagle* had landed on the *Sea of Tranquillity*. Hill and the Mexican woman who brought her the basil watched Neil Armstrong make that famous giant step for mankind. Later, the Mexican basil made a more modest footprint in the herb garden, becoming one of the first "flavored" basils to be sold by a large U.S. seed company. Park Seed's catalog has called the basil "cinnamon" since its introduction.

We grew several basils called "cinnamon". They all had distinctly veined, pointed green leaves 2 to 3¼ inches (5 to 8 cm) long and 1¼ to 1⅝ inches (3 to 4 cm) wide. Light lavender blossoms circle a 7-inch (18-cm) purple-stained flower stem. Plants may reach 36 inches (91 cm).

NORMALLY REPRODUCED FROM SEED.

TIMING: *At 70°F (21°C), germination is 3 days; transplant 14 days after sowing; garden ready 27 days after sowing.*

FIRST FLOWERING: *50 to 60 days from sowing.*

HEIGHT AT FIRST FLOWERING: *25 inches (63 cm).*

PAIRS OF LEAVES ON FLOWERING STEM: *7.*

WIDTH AT FIRST FLOWERING: *19 inches (48 cm).*

AROMA AND TASTE: *The clean spicy aroma combines cinnamon, sweet grass, mint and a trace of anise. Citrus zest and spice lend a perfumed taste that is followed by anise and mint tones, leaving a final warm pungency on the tongue. Cinnamon-scented methyl cinnamate dominates the essential oil but a significant portion is the floral-scented linalool.*

CLOVE.
Ocimum gratissimum 'Clove'. The African heritage of this plant is evident in its tall, stately bearing and straight, tan, woody stems. The plant is crowned with an unusual 7-inch (18-cm) plume of flower spikes, as many as seventeen spikes sprouting from a single stem. Flowers are small and white with tiny dark sepals. Leaves are heart-shaped, green, 2½ to 5½ inches (6 to 14 cm) long by 1¼ to 3¼ inches (3 to 8 cm) wide. They are heavily toothed at the margins and are heavily veined; surface is delicately fuzzed. The overall appearance of this plant in the landscape is regal and sparkling.

NORMALLY REPRODUCED FROM CUTTINGS.
HEIGHT AT FIRST FLOWERING: *36 inches (91 cm).*
PAIRS OF LEAVES ON FLOWERING STEM: *10.*
WIDTH AT FIRST FLOWERING: *10 inches (25 cm).*
AROMA AND TASTE: *There is some clove to the aroma, with definite camphorous compounds, and some spice and mint, creating a fragrance that is both sweet and musky. The taste is green, with camphor and mint tones. This is a great ornamental, but it won't win any taste competitions. The clove-scented eugenol makes up more than half the essential oil.*

CUBAN.
Ocimum basilicum 'Cuban'. This stately, columnar basil with showy, cone-shaped flower heads originated in Cuba. It made its way to the United States in a time-honored tradition, through immigrant gardeners who knew the value of their plants and wanted to preserve them. In this case, a Cuban woman gave seeds to an American couple in Florida. They sent the seed to their son, a Pennsylvania clergyman, Douglas Siedel, who has a passion for herbs. Siedel passed on the seeds to Cyrus and Louise Hyde who subsequently offered 'Cuban' through their Well-Sweep Herb Farm catalog.

Heart-shaped leaves 3/4 to 1 inch (2 to 2.5 cm) long by 7/16 to 1 inch (1 to 2.5 cm) wide fill the stiffly upright stems of this attention-getting basil. Leaf margins are only lightly and occasionally notched; stems are nearly hairless. The branched inflorescence begins life as a compact cone filled with white blossoms that open irregularly, then elongates to about 4 inches (10 cm) by the time of the last flower.

NORMALLY REPRODUCED FROM CUTTINGS.
HEIGHT AT FIRST FLOWERING: *22½ inches (57 cm).*
PAIRS OF LEAVES ON FLOWERING STEM: *15.*
WIDTH AT FIRST FLOWERING: *12 inches (30 cm).*
AROMA AND TASTE: *The leaves, when brushed, emit a sweet scent of cinnamon and cloves with a green basil roundness of mint and anise. The first taste is spice, followed by mint and a hint of anise. There is a definite pungency that makes the tip of the tongue slightly hot. The essential oil is dominated by floral-scented linalool and the spicy-camphorous 1,8-cineole.*

DARK OPAL.

DARK OPAL. *Ocimum* 'Dark Opal' (*O. basilicum* × *O. forskolei*). 'Dark Opal', the work of John Scarchuk and Joseph Lent, was a 1962 All-America Selection, the first herb so honored. Scarchuk and Lent began their work with seed gathered from wild populations in Turkey by U.S. Department of Agriculture plant explorers. From the diverse forms of basil produced by the Turkish seed on their plot at the University of Connecticut's Storres Agricultural Experiment Station, Scarchuk and Lent selected a single, dark purple-leaved plant. After several years, they had tamed the plant's genes sufficiently to achieve the uniformity they desired. They named it 'Dark Opal'. In the seed marketplace, 'Dark Opal' was the first to escape the narrow, largely unfamiliar confines of the herb garden and turn up in the mainstream spotlight. "It's a flower! It's an ornamental foliage plant! It's an herb!" was the way Ferry-Morse Seed Company introduced this new basil. The plant was unrivaled in the commercial seed world for a quarter century. At the same time, it became breeding material for amateurs and professionals alike.

Ferry-Morse's description of the foliage, while romantic, is accurate: "The foliage has the deep, almost black-purple of a purple plum. Over it, a bronzy-green sheen, iridescent, changes each time a breeze moves the leaves." Leaves are 2 to $3^{1}/_{4}$ inch (5 to 8 cm) long and $1^{1}/_{8}$ to $1^{3}/_{4}$ inch (3 to 4 cm) wide. Leaf margins are toothed. Strong light and fertile soil may bring out the darkest coloring. Blooms vary from plant to plant, running from pure white to deep fuchsia, usually with a lighter throat that contrasts beautifully with the dark purple bracts. Flower whorls are carried on 5-inch (13-cm) reddish-purple stems. The plant's hybrid parentage may cause its genetic instability when grown from seed; leaf color often varies from plant to plant and large numbers of pure green plants may be produced.

NORMALLY REPRODUCED BY CUTTINGS OR SEED.
TIMING: *At 70°F (21°C), germination is 3 days; transplant 14 days from sowing; garden ready 31 days from sowing.*
FIRST FLOWERING: *59 days from sowing.*
HEIGHT AT FIRST FLOWERING: *19 inches (48 cm).*
PAIRS OF LEAVES ON FLOWERING STEM: *9.*
WIDTH AT FIRST FLOWERING: *13 inches (33 cm).*
AROMA AND TASTE: *Dark Opal's murkiness blocks the usual clean, bright scents of basil.*

The aroma varies because of genetic instability but is generally crowned with a complex sweetness that consists of cinnamon, clove, mint, and anise with an herby finish. The taste is herby, spiked with citrus zest, followed by anise, a touch of spice, and mint. 'Dark Opal' has a slightly bitter aftertaste, as do most purple-leaved varieties. The flowery fragrance of linalool dominates the essential oil.

DWARF BOUQUET.

DWARF BOUQUET. *Ocimum* 'Dwarf Bouquet' (*O. basilicum* × *O. americanum*). This dainty-leaved bush basil originated too many years ago to identify its source, according to Cyrus Hyde, who has protected it from extinction; he believes it probably came from commercial seed he purchased. We considered 'Dwarf Bouquet' a real find, the smallest-leaved bush basil in our trials, but it is also a plant with little self-discipline. If left unpruned, its thin stems may become weak and rangy, although it still won't top 18 inches (46 cm).

This dwarf basil is an excellent ornamental that creates an alluring, soft mound of green topped by white stars. Its big sweet spicy aroma is a welcome surprise from such petite leaves. Heart-shaped with smooth margins that cup upwards, the leaves at their largest are 1/2 inch (1 cm) long and 1/4 inch (.5 cm) wide. Small white flowers circle 3-inch (7.5-cm) green flower stems. This basil will charm you out of your muddy boots.

NORMALLY REPRODUCED FROM CUTTINGS.
HEIGHT AT FIRST FLOWERING: *12 inches (30 cm).*
PAIRS OF LEAVES ON FLOWERING STEM: *10.*
WIDTH AT FIRST FLOWERING: *15 inches (38 cm).*
AROMA AND TASTE: *'Dwarf Bouquet' exudes a powerful, complex perfume when its leaves are stroked. Sweet smells of spice, cloves, and cinnamon, with a hint of vanilla, are followed by a tea-like scent of bergamot, citrus, and sweet anise. The taste is lavish, with tea and herb flavors, a spicy warmth, slightly resinous and bitter, a measure of anise, and a little mint. The scent derives from a complex mixture of chemicals but is dominated by the floral scent of linalool and to a lesser extent the spicy-scented β-caryophyllene.*

EAST INDIAN.

Ocimum gratissimum 'East Indian'. This basil originated in Zimbabwe and was introduced by Richters in 1982. The slender, woody-stemmed 'East Indian' basil is as unusual an ornamental herb as we have seen. Nearly four feet (122 cm) of stiff, tan stem carries green, heart-shaped leaves, many as large as 5½ inches (14 cm) long by 3¼ inches (8 cm) wide. Leaves are heavily toothed with prominent veining, the upper side is covered with a light fuzz. The flower heads are stunning and generous. Atop each stem are incredible clusters of 7-inch (18-cm) inflorescences filled with tiny lavender-tinged white blossoms, a kind of living bouquet.

NORMALLY REPRODUCED FROM SEED.
TIMING: *At 70°F (21°C), germination is 9 days; transplant 22 days after sowing; garden ready 36 days after sowing.*
FIRST FLOWERING: *69 days from sowing.*
HEIGHT AT FIRST FLOWERING: *42 inches (107 cm).*
PAIRS OF LEAVES ON FLOWERING STEM: *10.*
WIDTH AT FIRST FLOWERING: *10 inches (25 cm).*
AROMA AND TASTE: *Leaves are strong of spice with a cinnamon oil perfume. The flavor is more pungent and bitter than sweet basil and there is a resinous aftertaste. The scent derives from the clove scented eugenol and the floral-scented linalool.*

GENOA GREEN IMPROVED.

GENOA GREEN IMPROVED. *Ocimum basilicum* 'Genovese Verde Migliorato'. Our seed for this basil came directly from the Southern Italian province of Salerno. It purports to be the famous basil of Genoa and is a plant with which we have been familiar for well over a decade. Although it falls into the sweet basil category, we treat it separately because of its varietal characteristics which are honored in Italy. In America this variety may also be marketed as 'Genovese'.

Distinctive pointed green leaves are slightly puckered, strongly veined, and cupped by serrated margins that turn down. The average leaf length is $3\frac{1}{4}$ inches (8 cm) with a width of $1\frac{7}{8}$ inches (5 cm). Clear white flowers circle terminal stems that stretch to 6 inches (15 cm).

NORMALLY REPRODUCED FROM SEED.
TIMING: *At 70°F (21°C), germination is 3 days; transplant 12 days after sowing; garden ready 26 days after sowing.*
FIRST FLOWERING: *56 days from sowing.*
HEIGHT AT FIRST FLOWERING: *26 inches (66 cm).*
PAIRS OF LEAVES ON FLOWERING STEM: *7.*
WIDTH AT FIRST FLOWERING: *14 inches (36 cm).* AROMA AND TASTE: *A clean green aroma with anise hyssop, mint, and suggestions of citrus, cinnamon, and clove. A good rounded flavor is full of spice, licorice, and mint, with a subtle pungency. Genoa basil is a favorite for pesto in Italy and America. The essential oil is dominated by the floral-scented linalool, the spicy-scented β-caryophyllene, and the spicy-camphorous aroma of 1,8-cineole.*

GENOA PROFUMATISSIMA.

GENOA PROFUMATISSIMA. *Ocimum americanum* 'Genoa Profumatissima'. Of Italian origin, perfume basil debuted in several seed catalogs over the last decade and is justifiably popular. In appearance and growth habit, it is quite similar to Genoa green improved. We list it separately because it appears to be a different species with some flavor variation.

Perfume basil flaunts slightly puckered, strongly veined green leaves; margins are toothed and cupped. Leaves average $3\frac{1}{4}$ inches (8 cm) long and $1\frac{7}{8}$ inches (5 cm) wide. Stems are green with only a hint of hairiness; white flowers fill a 6-inch (15-cm) inflorescence.

NORMALLY REPRODUCED FROM SEED.
TIMING: *At 70°F (21°C), germination is 3 days; transplant 12 days after sowing; garden ready 26 days after sowing.*
FIRST FLOWERING: *56 days from sowing.*
HEIGHT AT FIRST FLOWERING: *26 inches (66 cm).*
PAIRS OF LEAVES ON FLOWERING STEM: *7.*
WIDTH AT FIRST FLOWERING: *14 inches (36 cm).* AROMA AND TASTE: *This variety has a lovely nose, a balance of citrus zest, licorice, cinnamon, spice, and mint. It is full-flavored as well, with citrus and anise predominating, followed by a spicy note. There is a little burning sensation from mint on the back of the palate. The essential oil is rich in the floral-scented linalool, the spicy-camphorous 1,8-cineole, and the clove-scented eugenol.*

GREEN.

GREEN. *Ocimum gratissimum* 'Green'. From a tiny seed with a humble name, this giant grows. 'Green' was far and away the tallest basil in our trials, reaching nearly 5 feet (1.5 m). Peter Borchard of Companion Plants in Athens, Ohio, has husbanded 'Green' for more than a decade. A taller version of 'Clove' and 'East Indian', it's a strikingly beautiful, willowy ornamental. Seven to nine flower stems mature at the same time on the tan, woody trunk and create inflorescences 4 inches (10 cm) long that are home to tiny, transparent, white blossoms carried in whorls. Oval leaves are dark green, heavily veined and well serrated; they average 6¼ inches (16 cm) long by 3¼ inches (8 cm) wide. The top side of the leaf is soft and delicately fuzzed. This is not a culinary herb, but is used in Africa for many medicinal purposes.

NORMALLY REPRODUCED FROM SEED.

TIMING: *At 70°F (21°C), germination is 4 days; transplant 15 days after sowing; garden ready 32 days after sowing.*

FIRST FLOWERING: *90 days from sowing.*

HEIGHT AT FIRST FLOWERING: *56 inches (142 cm).*

PAIRS OF LEAVES ON FLOWERING STEM: *10.*

WIDTH AT FIRST FLOWERING: *15½ inches (39 cm).*

AROMA AND TASTE: *The odor is musky and camphorous with some mint and anise. Its flavor is musky and resinous, a little like epazote. We consider this plant inedible but worth growing for its ornamental value.*

GREEN BOUQUET.

GREEN BOUQUET. *Ocimum* 'Green Bouquet', introduced in 1984, was the first of the new herbs—three basils, a dill, and a lavender—released from a large W. Atlee Burpee breeding program. The program was supervised by Ted C. Torrey and began in 1976 at the firm's research center in Santa Paula, California. Seed for 'Green Bouquet' derives from stock supplied to Burpee by Nichols Garden Nursery in Albany, Oregon.

Torrey's description of the plant as "a dwarf, almost boxwood type, small-leaved basil" is accurate, although it is on the tall side of "dwarf" at 18 inches (46 cm). The plant's stems are smooth and green, supporting pointed green leaves 1/2 to 5/8 inches (1 to 1.5 cm) long and 1/4 to 1/2 inches (.5 to 1 cm) wide. Leaves have light veining with some puckering; margins are smooth. Small to medium white blossoms are carried on a squat, cone-shaped flower head that elongates with age.

NORMALLY REPRODUCED FROM SEED.

TIMING: *At 70°F (21°C), germination is 3 days; transplant 12 days after sowing; garden ready 32 days after sowing.*

FIRST FLOWERING: *65 days from sowing.*

HEIGHT AT FIRST FLOWERING: *18 inches (46 cm).*

PAIRS OF LEAVES ON FLOWERING STEM: *6.*

WIDTH AT FIRST FLOWERING: *13 inches (33 cm).*

AROMA AND TASTE: *Resinous, oily, and flowery, the fragrance is an intense blend of spice, citrus, anise, and mint with a floral note. It is full of flavor, pungent of mint and anise, slightly herby, with cinnamon and clove. The chief constituents that comprise the essential oil are the floral-scented linalool, the clove-scented eugenol, and spice-scented β-caryophyllene.*

GREEN RUFFLES.

Ocimum 'Green Ruffles' (*O. basilicum* × *O. americanum*). 'Green Ruffles' is a unique lettuce-leaf basil produced by the enthusiasm of two talented people. In 1976 Ted Torrey, Burpee's long-time breeder, obtained seed samples from Helen Darrah, a Pennsylvania basil lover, collector, and subsequent author of *The Cultivated Basils*. Darrah's seeds were grown on a plot at Burpee's Santa Paula, California, facility under Torrey's experienced eyes. From a group of seeds Darrah had labeled "Curly", Torrey selected a single, unique plant that was introduced in 1987 as 'Green Ruffles'.

'Green Ruffles' has large green, oval leaves that are deeply toothed, heavily veined, and puckered; margins curl upward. Foliage averages 2½ to 3½ inches (6 to 9 cm) long by 2⅛ to 3¾ inches (5 to 9.5 cm) wide. Thick green lightly haired flower stems, average 6½ inches (16.5 cm) long and support whorls of white flowers. Calyxes are green and slightly hairy.

NORMALLY REPRODUCED FROM SEED.
TIMING: *At 70°F (21°C), germination is 3 days; transplant 13 days after sowing; garden ready 26 days after sowing.*
FIRST FLOWERING: *68 days from sowing.*
HEIGHT AT FIRST FLOWERING: *28 inches (71 cm).*
PAIRS OF LEAVES ON FLOWERING STEM: *6.*
WIDTH AT FIRST FLOWERING: *12 inches (30 cm).*

AROMA AND TASTE: *This large basil has a big, round, sweet aroma to match. The scent is strongly weighted with licorice and gently modified with mint and sweet hyacinth, plus a light accent of cinnamon. It tastes of sweet anise with strong mint overtones. Its overall effect: a sweet, mild, clean green salad herb. The scent derives from the anise-scented methyl chavicol and the floral-scented linalool.*

HOLY BASIL (INDIAN TULSI).

Ocimum tenuiflorum (*O. sanctum*). In its native India, holy basil grows wild, with green leaves or leaves tinged with purple. It is a plant group with considerable genetic diversity that provides aromatic variety. Individual clones have lemon, clove, anise, or a medicinal, spicy scent. Such plants are called chemotypes, a scientific distinction for look-alikes with differing scents.

The intricacies of morphology and chemistry cannot mask the reverence in which these basils are held, or their long and intimate association with the people of India and their dreams. Holy basil is a symbol of love and fidelity and is woven through many daily rituals. Touching and contemplation of the plant are said to free an individual from sin; washing the dead with basil water is believed to assure their entrance to heaven.

This unassuming, stiffly upright plant has pointed, elliptical foliage, light green or purple tinged. Leaves are 1¾ to 2½ inches (4.5 to 6 cm) long and 3/4 to 1½ inches (2 to 4 cm) wide. Green and purple-tinted stems are covered with fine hairs. Tiny magenta petals peek from under light green calyxes that wrap around single, 5-inch (13-cm) long terminal stems.

NORMALLY REPRODUCED FROM SEED.

TIMING: *At 70°F (21°C), germination is 7 days; transplant 21 days after sowing; garden ready 36 days after sowing.*

FIRST FLOWERING: *56 days from sowing.*

HEIGHT AT FIRST FLOWERING: *20 inches (51 cm).*

PAIRS OF LEAVES ON FLOWERING STEM: *8.*

WIDTH AT FIRST FLOWERING: *12 inches (30 cm).*

AROMA AND TASTE: *Holy basil has a delicate aroma of mint and camphor. The taste is green, minty, musky, and bitter, not the qualities of a culinary herb. The scent of our plants was dominated by the clove-scented eugenols and cinnamon-scented methyl cinnamate.*

HOLLY'S PAINTED.

Ocimum 'Holly's Painted' (*O. basilicum* × *O. americanum*). Frustrated in the spring of 1990 with all the green-leaved 'Purple Ruffles' seedlings that sprouted in his flats, Tom decided to look for the beauty that was there rather than what had been promised. 'Holly's Painted', introduced the next year, was a selection from those rogues. Its name honors Holly Shimizu of the U.S. Botanic Garden who has done so much to popularize herbs in North America.

Leaves are green, heart-shaped and strongly splashed with purple on both sides. Variegation fluctuates seasonally; on occasion the upper leaves become entirely purple. Leaves are $2\frac{1}{2}$ to $3\frac{3}{4}$ inches (6 to 9.5 cm) long and $1\frac{3}{4}$ to $2\frac{1}{2}$ inches (4 to 6 cm) wide, with margins strongly serrated. Medium-large flower petals, pink to light purple with a darker throat, stand out from slightly hairy bracts and calyxes that are green with a purple tint. Immature flower stems are 3 to 6 inches (8 to 15 cm); plants reach an ultimate height of 2 to 3 feet (61 to 91 cm). 'Holly's Painted' is a decorative garden accent that serves as a base for flower arrangements; it's also great in salads.

NORMALLY REPRODUCED FROM CUTTINGS.

HEIGHT AT FIRST FLOWERING: *17 inches (43 cm).*

PAIRS OF LEAVES ON FLOWERING STEM: *7.*

WIDTH AT FIRST FLOWERING: *12 inches (30 cm).*

AROMA AND TASTE: *The leaves have a strong, licorice scent with a hint of cinnamon; mint is absent. The sweet flavor combines anise with a little spice and a hint of mint. The scent derives from nearly equal amounts of floral-scented linalool and anise-scented methyl chavicol.*

ITALIAN, DWARF.   *Ocimum* 'Dwarf Italian' (*O. basilicum* × *O. americanum*). An old man from New Jersey who was born in Italy brought seeds of this basil to Cyrus Hyde of Well-Sweep Herb Farm. The devoted gardener had collected his basil seeds annually for sixty-five years. The light green leaves are elliptical, 1½ inches (4 cm) long and 7/8 inch (2 cm) wide. Foliage is not as dense as many bush basils'; white blossoms circle single flower stems.

NORMALLY REPRODUCED FROM SEED AND CUTTINGS.
HEIGHT AT FIRST FLOWERING: *15½ inches (39 cm).*
PAIRS OF LEAVES ON FLOWERING STEM: *5.*
WIDTH AT FIRST FLOWERING: *13 inches (33 cm).*
AROMA AND TASTE: *Sweet basil-like aroma with spice in the spotlight; spice and licorice guide the flavor. There is a hint of bitterness in the aftertaste. A large amount of the anise-scented methyl chavicol and a more moderate concentration of orange-flower-scented ocimene provide character to this essential oil.*

KARAMANOS.   *Ocimum basilicum* 'Karamanos'. Many years ago Christos and Popi Karamanos, friends of Tom's, returned from a visit home to Greece with basil seeds. This bounty produced a plant with pointed green leaves, lightly-veined, with subtle serration of the margins. Leaves average 1¼ inches (3 cm) long by 3/4 inch (2 cm) wide. White flowers that circle terminal stems are produced on a 5-inch (13-cm) inflorescence. Petals begin opening before the spike has cleared the leaf canopy.

NORMALLY REPRODUCED FROM SEED.
TIMING: *At 70°F (21°C), germination is 3 days; transplant 13 days after sowing; garden ready 25 days after sowing.*
FIRST FLOWERING: *51 days from sowing.*
HEIGHT AT FIRST FLOWERING: *17 inches (43 cm).*
PAIRS OF LEAVES ON FLOWERING STEM: *5.*
WIDTH AT FIRST FLOWERING: *17 inches (43 cm).*
AROMA AND TASTE: *The plant's scent is a deep, rich, mellow blending of cinnamon and clove with a subtle mixture of sweet hyacinth and a soft anise finish; no mint. Its taste combines anise, spice, and a cinnamon basil sweetness, with strong tea and green herb flavor. Not really hot, it does have a tongue-numbing effect.*

LEMON.

Ocimum 'Lemon' (*O. basilicum* × *O. americanum*). Although Gerard mentioned "Limon or Citron" in his sixteenth-century herbal, lemon basil didn't find its way to the United States in any significant way until 1940 when the U.S. Agriculture Department obtained seed from Thailand. It was first distributed in this country by Laurel Hill Herb Farm, owned by the legendary American herbalist Gertrude Foster and her husband Philip. Park Seed Co. began selling lemon basil seed nearly two decades ago, the first of the large mail-order seed merchants to do so; Park's seedline apparently came from Richard Dufresne who had purchased his seed from Heinz Grotzke's Meadowbrook Herb Garden in Wyoming, Rhode Island.

Many seed merchants offer lemon basil today, but most seed is sold under the unmodified rubric "lemon basil". Only Shepherd's Garden Seeds more closely identifies its lemon offering as "Maenglak Thai", a seed that is produced in Thailand. The plants from all merchants appear nearly identical.

Lemon basil's egg-shaped, light green leaves are 2¼ to 3¼ inches (6 to 8 cm) long by 1⅛ to 1½ inches (3 to 4 cm) wide; they are delicately veined with nearly smooth margins. Stems are slightly fuzzed. Smallish white blossoms are carried in whorls on 12-inch (30-cm) stems. Plants reach 26 to 30 inches (66 to 76 cm) high and 19 inches (48 cm) wide at maturity when left unpinched.

NORMALLY REPRODUCED FROM SEED.

TIMING: At 70°F (21°C), germination is 3 days; transplant 14 days after sowing; garden ready 26 days after sowing.

FIRST FLOWERING: 46 days from sowing.

HEIGHT AT FIRST FLOWERING: 16½ inches (42 cm).

PAIRS OF LEAVES ON FLOWERING STEM: 6.

WIDTH AT FIRST FLOWERING: 10 inches (25 cm).

AROMA AND TASTE: In most lemon basils, lemon-balm scent dominates the aroma; spice and mint come through with minor notes of anise and musk. The taste is oily, lemon with floral tones, though slightly flat and reminiscent of green tea, with a zing of mint. Maenglak Thai Lemon is a more complex blend, lemon followed by spice with a touch of musk, then clove and cinnamon; there is barely a hit of camphor, some anise and mint. Maenglak Thai Lemon has a pleasant, oily lemon flavor that is flowery, just slightly hot and spicy, with a little bitterness. In all lemon basils, the chief ingredient in the essential oil is the lemon-scented citral with minor amounts of floral-scented linalool and spicy-scented β-caryophyllene.

LEMON, MRS. BURNS'.

Ocimum basilicum 'Mrs. Burns' Lemon'. Native Seeds Search, a preservationist organization in Tucson, Arizona, introduced this strongly-scented lemon basil at the behest of one of its founders, Barney Burns, whose mother Janet had grown it for more than thirty years. A Canadian, Mrs. Burns moved to Carlsbad, New Mexico in 1939 and soon met a local woman, Mrs. Clifton, who gave her the lemon basil seed. Mrs. Clifton had grown it since the 1920s. The Burns family had an unusual way of enjoying lemon basil. According to Mr. Burns, he and his mother invented Barney's Basil Burger, a combination of ground beef and finely chopped lemon basil, cooked on an outdoor grill. Janet Burns died in 1985.

'Mrs. Burns' grows into a plant larger than other lemon basils, easily 3 feet (91 cm) tall. While its green stems appear smooth, fingers can feel a light covering of fuzz. Long, pointed, elliptical green leaves are 3½ inches (4 cm) long and 1⅞ inches (5 cm) wide, strongly veined with wavy margins. Pink-tinged white flowers with long sepals dance in rings around terminal 5- to 10-inch (13- to 25-cm) inflorescences.

NORMALLY REPRODUCED FROM SEED.
TIMING: *At 70°F (21°C), germination is 3 days; transplant 13 days after sowing; garden ready 26 days after sowing.*
FIRST FLOWERING: *57 days from sowing.*
HEIGHT AT FIRST FLOWERING: *30½ inches (77 cm).*
PAIRS OF LEAVES ON FLOWERING STEM: *8.*

WIDTH AT FIRST FLOWERING: *21 inches (53 cm).*
AROMA AND TASTE: *The big lemon aroma of 'Mrs. Burns' is resinous and oily, followed by spicy cinnamon with a floral note. The clean, strong lemon zest taste is backed with light spice and mint. The scent derives from the floral notes of linalool and lemon-scented citral.*

LESBOS.

Ocimum 'Lesbos'. A chance encounter in a Greek-American diner bore interesting consequences for basil lovers. The Reverend Douglas Siedel met the diner's owner, talked herbs, and left with a double feeling of satisfaction—a full stomach and some basil seeds from Greece. Siedel shared the seeds with the Hydes at their Well-Sweep Herb Farm in New Jersey and the result was 'Lesbos', an unusual stately basil with small leaves.

Two other basils similar to 'Lesbos', 'Aussie Sweetie' and 'Greek Column', are also the offspring of casual encounters. Both herbs came into Tom's possession about 1989, 'Aussie Sweetie' in plant form from a customer at his nursery, and 'Greek Column' from Michael Soteriou who brought the seed from a plant in his sister's garden on Cyprus. The 'Aussie Sweetie' plant had been grown from seed purchased in Australia by a vacationer, but attempts to locate the seed in the Australian herb trade have been fruitless. Tom gave different names to his basils because 'Greek Column' is more rigidly upright than 'Aussie Sweetie'. Both may share the same Greek gene pool with 'Lesbos'; the essential oil chemistry of 'Aussie Sweetie' and 'Lesbos' are quite similar. ('Greek Column' was not tested.)

Tom theorizes that the Australian seed may have found its way south with Greek immigrants. In addition to a common form and aroma, all three basils share a unique characteristic: they do not flower during the long days of summer. Unlike most basils, these three bloom sparsely and, where conditions permit, set seed in the fall and winter. Whether the slight differences among these three plants warrant different names is a taxonomic decision for the experts. Until such a decision is made (and unless the plant has another, earlier Greek name) 'Lesbos' probably has priority because it was the first name given.

These three basils share a columnar growth habit, standing 3 to 4 feet (91 to 122 cm) high, depending on the length of the growing season. They have medium-green, heart-shaped leaves, clearly veined, with barely toothed margins. Leaves are 1½ inches (4 cm) long by 1⅛ inches (3 cm) wide. Stems are lightly fuzzed. The first half-inch or so of the stems is tinted light purple. Plants may require staking if branches are left unpruned.

NORMALLY REPRODUCED FROM CUTTINGS.
HEIGHT AT FIRST FLOWERING: *36 to 48 inches (91 to 122 cm)*.
PAIRS OF LEAVES ON FLOWERING STEM: NA.
WIDTH AT FIRST FLOWERING: *24 inches (61 cm)*.
AROMA AND TASTE: *One of the most complex basil aromas, and the strongest. The first sniff is loaded with cinnamon and has a background of allspice and cloves; this is followed by anise* *and sweet fruit. Pumpkin-pie spice comes to mind. The flavor is full of spice, citrus, a slight grassiness, and a hint of warm anise, leaving a perfumed taste. Cinnamate is the dominate chemical in the essential oil, but the floral-scented linalool, the clove-scented methyl eugenol, and the spicy-camphorous 1,8-cineole are also major players.*

LETTUCE LEAF.

Ocimum basilicum. Basils with super large leaves are often said to have "lettuce leaves", puckered here, smooth there. Most lettuce-leaf basils look and act alike, no matter their name. This is the grab bag of the basil garden, the place you go when you want a lot of basil but aren't particular, as long as the leaves are big and sweet. We tested six basils called "lettuce leaf", a large sweet, a large green, a green broadleaf, a 'Napoletano', a 'Mammoth', and a 'Valentino'. Although the latter three bore names, they displayed so much variation (from puckered to smooth, for instance) that we decided they were lettuce-leaf basils at heart, just dressed fancier.

Our lettuce-leaf basils all had green foliage that averaged 5 to 6½ inches (13 to 16.5 cm) long and 3⅜ to 4 inches (9 to 10 cm) wide. Some leaves were robustly puckered, others smooth; all margins were serrated. Large white flowers were carried on inflorescences 6 to 7 inches (15 to 18 cm) long; the typical circles of blossoms around the flower stem were sometimes close together, often loosely spaced. All calyxes and bracts were green and hairy.

NORMALLY REPRODUCED FROM SEED.
TIMING: *At 70°F (21°C), germination is 3 days; transplant 12 days after sowing; garden ready 26 days after sowing.*
FIRST FLOWERING: *60 days from sowing.*
HEIGHT AT FIRST FLOWERING: *25 to 30 inches (63 to 76 cm)*.
PAIRS OF LEAVES ON FLOWERING STEM: *7*.
WIDTH AT FIRST FLOWERING: *14 to 18 inches (36 to 46 cm)*.

AROMA AND TASTE: *The odor of these large leaves is licorice sweet, herby green with a bit of mint and a finishing note of cinnamon. They taste of licorice with just a touch of mint and cinnamon. Lettuce-leaf basil is uncomplicated, robust, excellent in salads, sauces, and tossed with tomatoes and olive oil. There was some variation in the essential oils but all were high in anise-scented methyl chavicol and the floral-scented linalool.*

MEXICAN SPICE.

MEXICAN SPICE. *Ocimum basilicum* 'Mexican Spice'. The seed for this handsome basil originated in Mexico, according to Rosemarie Nichols McGee of Nichols Garden Nursery. Stem tips tend to be ruby colored, a nice contrast to the heart-shaped, light green leaves. Well-veined with some puckering, the leaves are 2⅜ inches (6 cm) long by 1½ inches (4 cm) wide. Light pink flowers peek from under purple calyxes and are carried around a purple-tinted stem. The inflorescence is 3½ to 7 inches (9 to 18 cm).

NORMALLY REPRODUCED FROM SEED.
TIMING: *At 70°F (21°C), germination is 3 days; transplant 14 days after sowing; garden ready 26 days after sowing.*
FIRST FLOWERING: *50 days from sowing.*
HEIGHT AT FIRST FLOWERING: *26½ inches (67 cm).*
PAIRS OF LEAVES ON FLOWERING STEM: *7.*
WIDTH AT FIRST FLOWERING: *18 inches (46 cm).*

AROMA AND TASTE: *A clean, spicy aroma combines cinnamon, sweet grass, mint, and a trace of anise. Citrus and spice oils lend a perfumey taste with some anise and mint tones, and a final warm pungency on the tongue. The essential oil is high in floral-scented linalool with a modest amount of anise-scented methyl chavicol.*

MINIATURE.

MINIATURE. *Ocimum* 'Miniature'. Twenty-five years ago a now-anonymous member of the Herb Society of America shared a basil cutting with Cyrus Hyde of Well-Sweep Herb Farm in New Jersey, thereby ensuring the perpetuation of this globe-shaped, small-leaved basil. It is likely the original came from seed sold by the Fosters, Hills, or Chalfins. The freely-branching plant has thick stems that provide strong support for its dense growth and appealing globe shape; it is quite distinct from bush basils grown from commercial seed. 'Miniature' is the perfect plant to soften the hard edges of small rectilinear gardens or to provide a graceful annual hedge for large spaces.

Leaves on this short basil are dark green and pointed with lightly toothed margins, averaging 1 inch (2.5 cm) long and 3/4 inch (2 cm) wide. Ruffled, small white flowers with long sepals adorn 4-inch (10-cm) single stems. The flowers begin opening before the inflorescences have poked through the dense mound of foliage.

NORMALLY REPRODUCED FROM CUTTINGS.
HEIGHT AT FIRST FLOWERING: *12 inches (30 cm).*
PAIRS OF LEAVES ON FLOWERING STEM: *9.*
WIDTH AT FIRST FLOWERING: *11½ inches (29 cm).*
AROMA AND TASTE: *The aroma of this plant departs from the traditional. It's spicy, citrus with a touch of mint, cinnamon with a suggestion of anise. A hot and pungent sensation greets the tongue and is followed by an oily, resinous flavor of spicy cinnamon and mint, with a bitter aftertaste. The essential oil is an interesting combination of floral-scented linalool, spicy-camphorous 1,8-cineole, spicy-scented β-caryophyllene, and camphor.*

MINIATURE PUERTO RICAN.

Ocimum basilicum 'Miniature Puerto Rican'. A decade ago New Jersey herb breeder Cyrus Hyde developed 'Miniature Puerto Rican' by crossing two basils in his large collection, the dainty-leaved 'Miniature' and the larger-leaved 'Puerto Rican'. He got an ample, late-blooming basil with small leaves and a lovely branched flower head.

'Miniature Puerto Rican' is medium tall, holding small, fragrant heart-shaped leaves with margins that are smooth to slightly toothed; the surface is lightly veined. Leaves are 3/4 to 1⅛ inches (2 to 3 cm) long and 3/8 to 7/8 inch (1 to 2 cm) wide. Large white blossoms burst from a dense cone of compressed flower stems 3 to 4 inches (8 to 10 cm) long. The plant is typically somewhat flattened across its broad top.

NORMALLY REPRODUCED FROM CUTTINGS.
HEIGHT AT FIRST FLOWERING: *23 inches (58 cm).*
PAIRS OF LEAVES ON FLOWERING STEM: *15.*
WIDTH AT FIRST FLOWERING: *20 inches (51 cm).*
AROMA AND TASTE: *The leaves' aroma is full of spice, oily and slightly resinous, with cinnamon, mint, anise, and a sweet, flowery finish.*

The flavor is pungent, bitter and spicy, with some mint and green herb undertones. The essential oil is high in cinnamon-scented cinnamate and also has significant amounts of flowery-scented linalool and the spicy-camphorous 1,8-cineole.

MINIATURE PURPLE, WELL-SWEEP.

Ocimum basilicum 'Well-Sweep Miniature Purple'. Cyrus Hyde of Well-Sweep Herb Farm took an Armenian basil with a small rounded shape and tiny pointed leaves and crossed it with 'Dark Opal'. Hyde was inspired by a description of an obsolete, small-leaved purple basil grown by noted American herbalist Gertrude Foster. He got a few small-leaved purple basil plants but he was unable to stabilize seed. Helen Darrah had seed for a green-leaved basil with purple flower bracts that Hyde then crossed with his dwarf purple. He liked the result, but his selected line remains unstable and must be propagated from cuttings.

'Well-Sweep Miniature Purple' grows into a colorful purple mound topped with a burst of light lavender blooms; the elongated ball-shaped flower head, averages 2 inches (5 cm) long by 1½ inches (4 cm) wide. This striking annual shrublet is 12 to 16 inches (30 to 41 cm) high. Cuttings, when pinched back several times, mature into rounded plants about 12 inches (30 cm) wide. Leaves are pointed, egg-shaped, and their margins are lightly serrated; they average 1 inch (2.5 cm) long and 5/8 inch (1.5 cm) wide. As leaves age, the depth of color fades and the resulting glaze of purple over green gives them an iridescence similar to 'Dark Opal'. Leaf undersides and stems are reddish purple. The plant displays soft charm in the landscape.

REPRODUCED BY ROOTED CUTTINGS.
HEIGHT AT FIRST FLOWERING: *12 inches (30 cm).*
PAIRS OF LEAVES ON FLOWERING STEM: *6.*
WIDTH AT FIRST FLOWERING: *12 inches (30 cm).*
AROMA AND TASTE: *Tiny leaves exude a sweet, spicy scent with minor notes of cinnamon and mint; it's a fragrance similar to that of 'Dark*

Opal' but round, with more sparkle. On the tongue, the leaf is aromatic, oily, with cinnamon and mint, some herb, and a slight bitterness. The essential oil is rich in floral-scented linalool along with the spicy-camphorous 1,8-cineole.

NAPOLETANO.

Ocimum basilicum 'Napoletano'. This sweet basil, a standard in southern Italy, captures the robust, outgoing spirit of Naples. Although it is very large-leaved and could be categorized as a lettuce-leaf, its uniform varietal characteristics separate it from its generic brethren. We purchased the seed for this variety in Italy.

In our trials, it had the most rippled leaves of any large-leaved basil; the super-large, light green leaves are puckered like a crocodile's skin and heavily veined. This basil has the look of a prehistoric plant, one you can easily imagine growing in the Garden of Eden. The average leaf is elongated but some leaves are truncated. Typical leaves are 4½ to 5¾ inches (11 to 15 cm) long by 3¾ to 5 inches (9.5 to 13 cm) wide; the serrated margins (also puckered) turn under. Large, white flowers are carried in whorls on stiff, unbranched stems. Bracts and calyxes are green and quite fuzzy.

NORMALLY REPRODUCED FROM SEED.
TIMING: *At 70°F (21°C), germination is 3 days; transplant 12 days after sowing; garden ready 27 days after sowing.*
FIRST FLOWERING: *62 days from sowing.*
HEIGHT AT FIRST FLOWERING: *21 inches (53 cm).*
PAIRS OF LEAVES ON FLOWERING STEM: *6.*
WIDTH AT FIRST FLOWERING: *13 inches (33 cm).*

AROMA AND TASTE: *This large basil carries a sweet anise aroma with a touch of mint and a trace of herb. Its overpowering aroma is more muted on the tongue with anise and mint faintly in the background. It's an excellent salad and sauce basil. The scent derives from the floral-scented linalool and the richly anise-scented methyl chavicol with some minor notes of spicy-camphorous 1,8-cineole.*

NEW GUINEA.

Ocimum basilicum 'New Guinea'. Kim Kuebel, an avid Texas herb collector, is responsible for bringing 'New Guinea' basil to the attention of herb growers in the United States. Kuebel obtained his seed in 1980 from English botanist John K. Morton, a professor at the University of Waterloo in Canada. A precise man of few words, Morton could not remember sending the seeds to Kuebel nor where they came from, but he speculates that a European colleague, since deceased, may have shared seeds collected in New Guinea.

'New Guinea' is a colorful plant with green, arrow-shaped leaves suffused with dark purple. Leaf veins and undersides are also purple. The pointed leaves are 1½ to 2 inches (4 to 5 cm) long and 1/2 to 3/4 inches (1 to 2 cm) wide. Small light violet flowers, marked with purple splashes, are carried in whorls around 4- to 6-inch (10- to 15-cm) purple stems.

NORMALLY REPRODUCED FROM SEED AND CUTTING.
TIMING: *At 70°F (21°C), germination is 3 days; transplant 17 days after sowing; garden ready 32 days after sowing.*
FIRST FLOWERING: *60 days from sowing.*
HEIGHT AT FIRST FLOWERING: *17 inches (43 cm).*
PAIRS OF LEAVES ON FLOWERING STEM: *6.*
WIDTH AT FIRST FLOWERING: *18 inches (46 cm).*

AROMA AND TASTE: *There is nothing small about this basil's aroma. It releases a strong, sweet licorice odor with some mint and spice. The licorice flavor is sweet and potent, followed by mint and cinnamon, with a suggestion of flowers. The essential oil has a huge helping of anise-scented methyl chavicol.*

OSMIN.
Ocimum 'Osmin'. A richly colored purple-leaved basil, 'Osmin' made its U.S. debut in the 1996 catalog of Johnny's Selected Seeds. This new basil is the first offspring of a massive basil breeding program begun in 1987 at the Quedlinberg Research Station, about 100 miles southwest of Berlin in the former East Germany. More than 300 basils were gathered from around the world for the project. 'Osmin' is named after a character in Mozart's comic opera *Die Entfuhrüng Aus dem Serail (The Abduction from the Seraglio)*.

Although our experience with this new variety is limited, the breeding work appears nearly flawless. There are virtually no green offspring in the seedling flat, and leaves are an even, dark purple. Stems are slightly lighter in color and end with a 3-inch (8-cm) deeply colored inflorescence decorated with mauve blossoms. The dark leaves are heart-shaped with margins turned under slightly. The leaves are 2½ inches (6 cm) long and 1½ inches (4 cm) wide with deeply toothed margins.

NORMALLY REPRODUCED FROM SEED.

TIMING: *At 70°F (21°C), germination is 3 days; transplant 16 days after sowing; garden ready 30 days after sowing.*

FIRST FLOWERING: *69 days from sowing.*

HEIGHT AT FIRST FLOWERING: *12 inches (30 cm).*

PAIRS OF LEAVES ON FLOWERING STEM: *7.*

WIDTH AT FIRST FLOWERING: *8 inches (20 cm).*

AROMA AND TASTE: *The aroma is subtle and delicate with early notes of cinnamon followed by cloves and sweet vanilla with a hint of anise and mint. The flavor is also mild with a slight initial bitterness succeeded by a predominent green herbal taste. There is a hint of spice and the aftertaste is slightly bitter with some mint. The tongue is left numb, a bit like its reaction to tarragon.*

PERUVIAN.
Ocimum campechianum (formerly *O. micranthum*). This attractive little basil is native to Peru and appears in other south and central American countries, as well as Mexico and southern Florida. Leaves are dark green, prominently toothed and strongly veined, 2¼ to 3½ inches (6 to 9 cm) long and 1½ to 2 inches (4 to 5 cm) wide. Tiny light lavender blossoms circle green terminal stems. Inflorescences are decorative and come in threes. Plants may reach 2 feet (61 cm).

NORMALLY REPRODUCED FROM SEED.

TIMING: *At 70°F (21°C), germination is 5 days; transplant 15 days after sowing; garden ready 25 days after sowing.*

FIRST FLOWERING: *50 days from sowing.*

HEIGHT AT FIRST FLOWERING: *10½ inches (27 cm).*

PAIRS OF LEAVES ON FLOWERING STEM: *5.*

WIDTH AT FIRST FLOWERING: *11½ inches (29 cm).*

AROMA AND TASTE: *Leaves offer a savory, spicy aroma, not sweet but musky, with oregano highlights and a touch of mint and camphor. The pungent-green herb taste is resinous with some mint and ginger, and slightly bitter. It will never be a workhorse in the kitchen, but does enliven beans and salsa. The essential oil is rich in the spicy-camphorous 1,8-cineole, clove-scented eugenol, and cinnamon-scented cinnamate.*

PICCOLO.

Ocimum basilicum 'Piccolo'. The varietal name we've attached to this small-leaved Italian basil comes from Italian seed catalogs, where it is called *basilico piccolo verde fino*. The seed is available from a number of sources in Italy and has an ardent following there, due doubtless to its sweetly perfumed leaves and compact stature. The plant may be a breeding improvement of the rather lanky, small-leaved French basil known in North America as 'Sweet Fine'. 'Piccolo' has been available in the United States for at least a decade, but on a limited basis.

"Piccolo" means *little* in Italian, and while this basil is too tall to be regarded as a bush basil, it is compact for its size. Its medium-green leaves are glossy with light veining and gently toothed margins; they are carried on green stems that bear a hint of fine hair. Foliage is 3/4 to 1 inch (2 to 2.5 cm) long and 3/8 to 1/2 inch (.75 to 1 cm) wide. White medium-sized blossoms are carried in whorls around a green stem 4¹⁄₂ inches (11 cm) long. Regular pruning, a delightful duty with this basil, strengthens slender stems and decreases height.

NORMALLY REPRODUCED FROM SEED.
TIMING: **At 70°F (21°C), germination is 3 days; transplant 14 days after sowing; garden ready 29 days after sowing.**
FIRST FLOWERING: **65 days from sowing.**
HEIGHT AT FIRST FLOWERING: **21 inches (53 cm).**
PAIRS OF LEAVES ON FLOWERING STEM: **9.**
WIDTH AT FIRST FLOWERING: **18 inches (46 cm).**

AROMA AND TASTE: **The leaves produce a mild basil aroma that is spicy with a minty interlude and a touch of anise for a finale. The flavor is pungently spicy with herbal overtones, not too strong, with undertones of mint. The scent derives from the flowery linalool and the clove-scented eugenol.**

PUERTO RICAN.

Ocimum 'Puerto Rican' (*O. basilicum* × *O. americanum*). American missionaries in Puerto Rico brought the seeds of this basil to their New Jersey friends, Cy and Louise Hyde of Well-Sweep Herb Farm. The Hydes have protected the plant's genetic integrity for many years by producing offspring with rooted cuttings, although 'Puerto Rican' will doubtless reproduce well from seed.

This unusual basil has a somewhat flattened top from which green cones rise. The cones are packed with short stems full of large white blossoms. The effect is dramatic. The cones are noticeable when they are about 3/4 inch (2 cm) tall and elongate as the flowers open into 5-inch (13-cm) branched inflorescences. Leaves are medium green, clearly veined, and egg-shaped, averaging 2¹⁄₂ inches (6 cm) long by 1¹⁄₂ inches (4 cm) wide; margins are toothed and turn upward, giving leaves a cupped look.

NORMALLY REPRODUCED FROM CUTTINGS.
HEIGHT AT FIRST FLOWERING: **15 inches (38 cm).**
PAIRS OF LEAVES ON FLOWERING STEM: **8.**
WIDTH AT FIRST FLOWERING: **19¹⁄₂ inches (50 cm).**
AROMA AND TASTE: **A mellow, yet spicy, cinnamon aroma greets the nose and is followed by mint and anise, then floral notes. The leaves taste pungent, oily and resinous, with emphasis on the cinnamon; they're hot on the tongue, with mint and an insinuation of anise. The essential oil is dominated by the cinnamon-scented methyl cinnamate and the floral-scented linalool.**

PURPLE RUFFLES.

PURPLE RUFFLES. *O. basilicum* 'Purple Ruffles'. 'Purple Ruffles', a 1987 All America Selection, comes from a large herb-breeding program conducted by Ted Torrey at Burpee's Santa Paula, California facility. The plant results from a cross that Torrey made in 1980 of 'Green Ruffles', and 'Dark Opal'.

'Purple Ruffles' is a robust, showy basil bred for its ornamental value, but it's not without aromatic charm. Often treated as a bold accent in the garden, especially when paired with green or silver herbs, its leaves are a stunning dark purple (with some marginal greening), elliptical in shape with heavily serrated margins that maintain a slight upward curl. They are 3 inches (7.5 cm) long and 1¾ inches (4.5 cm) wide, heavily ribbed with moderate puckering. Medium-large flowers are carried on strong, dark purple stems that extend to 5 inches (13 cm). Blooms vary from white to light lavender with a dark fuchsia throat; blossom variation is a sign of this basil's genetic instability. Bracts and calyxes are dark purple and fuzzy.

We grew 'Purple Ruffles' from four sources and discovered considerable variation in the plants produced. One seed sample was highly contaminated with green and green-purple variegated seedlings. Whereas most of our flats produced 130 usable seedlings, this seed produced only 16 true-to-name seedlings. Such incidents cause fears that the 'Purple Ruffles' seedline is drifting into extinction, but even as we write, a number of breeders are conducting rescue efforts.

NORMALLY REPRODUCED FROM SEED, BUT CUTTINGS SEEM ADVISABLE BECAUSE OF SEED-LINE VARIATION.

TIMING: *At 70°F (21°C), germination is 3 days; transplant 18 days after sowing; garden ready 36 days after sowing.*

FIRST FLOWERING: *95 days from sowing.*

HEIGHT AT FIRST FLOWERING: *27 inches (69 cm).*

PAIRS OF LEAVES ON FLOWERING STEM: *12.*

WIDTH AT FIRST FLOWERING: *17 inches (43 cm).*

AROMA AND TASTE: *Nice round, sweet cinnamon-spice scent with some mint and anise. The taste is rather undefined, bland, herblike, with a hint of cinnamon. Fragrance and taste varied from plant to plant, probably because of genetic insecurity. The scent derives from significant amounts of the floral-scented linalool, spicy-scented β-caryophyllene, and anise-scented methyl chavicol.*

RED RUBIN.

RED RUBIN. *Ocimum* 'Red Rubin' (*O. basilicum* × *O. forskolei*). 'Red Rubin' is a gift from Denmark, an unlikely place for the production of a heat-loving, tropical plant, but such challenges have often intrigued Danish horticulturists. Whereas most basil seeds are gathered from plants in open fields, 'Red Rubin' seed has been produced since 1992 under strict control inside glass greenhouses. Unlike 'Dark Opal' and 'Purple Ruffles', it produces few plants with green leaves, probably the result of Danish care and indoor breeding.

'Red Rubin' has visual similarities to 'Dark Opal' but they're probably superficial. According to Janika Eckert of Johnny's Seeds, our liaison with the Danish firm that developed the new variety, breeding and selection of 'Red Rubin' began in the late

1980s with 'Red Ruffles', an old purple variety. The breeders' aim was to achieve a smooth-leaved plant with increased vigor.

The purple, egg-shaped leaves of 'Red Rubin' have toothed margins that are $3\frac{1}{4}$ inches (8 cm) long and $1\frac{3}{4}$ inches (4.5 cm) wide. As the leaves age, hints of green show through. Deep pink blossoms with violet throats spin around a 3-inch (8-cm) long terminal stem. Bracts and calyxes are purple with a bit of fuzz.

NORMALLY REPRODUCED FROM SEED.

TIMING: *At 70°F (21°C), germination is 3 days; transplant 12 days after sowing; garden ready 30 days after sowing.*

FIRST FLOWERING: *53 days from sowing.*

HEIGHT AT FIRST FLOWERING: *24 inches (61 cm).*

PAIRS OF LEAVES ON FLOWERING STEM: *9.*

WIDTH AT FIRST FLOWERING: *$15\frac{1}{2}$ inches (39 cm).*

AROMA AND TASTE: *Cinnamon-scented leaves have a slight perfume of mint and anise. The flavor is mild, indistinct, bland and herbal. The essential oil is high in floral-scented linalool, spicy-scented β-caryophyllene, and spicy-camphorous 1,8-cineole.*

SACRED.

Ocimum americanum 'Sacred'. This basil was a Richters' introduction before 1979 and we found no others like it in our trials. Conrad Richter says the source of the firm's seed was in India but this basil differs markedly from *O. tenuiflorum*, commonly called 'Holy' in the United States and 'Tulsi' in northern India.

'Sacred' basil is an effortlessly charming, light green, compact plant shaped like a tidy globe, almost as wide as it is tall, with an ultimate height about 17 inches (43 cm). Green stems appear smooth but bracts and calyxes are fuzzed. Elliptical leaves are $1\frac{3}{8}$ to $1\frac{3}{4}$ inches (3.5 to 4.5 cm) long and 5/8 to 1 inch (1.5 to 2.5 cm) wide, rather smooth with almost unpuckered margins. Tiny white flowers with red-streaked sepals are carried in whorls on thin terminal spikes, tinted light purple, that grow to $5\frac{1}{2}$ inches (14 cm). 'Sacred' was the only plant in our trials so intent on flowering that heavy pruning could not induce it to produce more foliage.

NORMALLY REPRODUCED FROM SEED.

TIMING: *At 70°F (21°C), germination is 6 days; transplant 15 days after sowing; garden ready 27 days after sowing.*

FIRST FLOWERING: *38 days from sowing.*

HEIGHT AT FIRST FLOWERING: *$11\frac{1}{2}$ inches (29 cm).*

PAIRS OF LEAVES ON FLOWERING STEM: *5.*

WIDTH AT FIRST FLOWERING: *11 inches (28 cm).*

AROMA AND TASTE: *The leaves of this basil hold bouquets of citrus, mint, and spice. Chewed, the leaves produce a citrus flavor, then a pungent, hot mint, with more perfume than spice. The scent derives from the cumin-thyme-scented cadinene, the spicy-scented β-caryophyllene, and the clove-scented methyl eugenol.*

SPICE. *Ocimum americanum* 'Spice'. A subject of confusion in the seed trade, this basil is hardly ever offered under its proper name, but as 'Sacred' or 'Holy' basil. While sacred or holy to some, it is not the Hindu holy basil (*O. tenuiflorum*, formerly called *O. sanctum*). Its misidentification may have occurred during the circuitous route it took to reach the mainstream.

Richard Dufresne transmitted the seed to Park Seed Company, who introduced it to a wider audience. Dufresne says he got the seed nearly twenty years ago from Heinz Grotzke, the founder of Meadowbrook Herb Garden in Rhode Island. Grotzke called his seed "Holy basil" and said it had come from a German source.

At maturity, 'Spice' basil may reach 20 inches (51 cm). Its distinctive heart-shaped green leaves are fuzzed and strongly veined with toothed margins. Leaves average 2 to 2½ inches (5 to 6 cm) long by 1¼ to 1¾ inches (3 to 4.5 cm) wide. Small, light violet blossoms are carried in whorls on hairy stems 5 to 6 inches (13 to 15 cm) long.

NORMALLY REPRODUCED FROM SEED.
TIMING: *At 70°F (21°C), germination is 4 days; transplant 15 days after sowing; garden ready 27 days after sowing.*
FIRST FLOWERING: *45 days from sowing.*
HEIGHT AT FIRST FLOWERING: *12 inches (30 cm).*
PAIRS OF LEAVES ON FLOWERING STEM: *7.*
WIDTH AT FIRST FLOWERING: *11½ inches (29 cm).*
AROMA AND TASTE: *Leaves exude a musky sweetness that fades to cinnamon and spice, with a slightly pungent note, and finishes with a mild, floral note. Perfume flavor fills the mouth at first bite, followed by mint, and is hot on the tongue. It's hard to believe anyone would eat this basil, but it is good for a patio tub or potpourri. The scent derives from the spicy-camphorous 1,8-cineole, clove-scented eugenol and the anise-scented methyl chavicol present in the plant's essential oil.*

SPICY BUSH. *Ocimum* 'Spicy Bush'. The branching habit of bush basils is the key to their pleasant, rounded shapes and 'Spicy Bush' exemplifies this characteristic perfectly. Branches and main stem appear to reach the same length simultaneously, creating a globe-shaped bush. 'Spicy Bush' has green leaves with light veining and serrated margins; leaves average 1¼ inches (3 cm) long by 5/8 inch (2 cm) wide. As with all basils, the first flowers open at the base of the short inflorescences and may go unseen. Ultimately, large white flowers spin around the flower stem, widely spaced as they climb 3½ inches (9 cm) to the top.

NORMALLY REPRODUCED FROM SEED.
TIMING: *At 70°F (21°C), germination is 3 days; transplant 15 days after sowing; garden ready 25 days after sowing.*
FIRST FLOWERING: *62 days from sowing.*
HEIGHT AT FIRST FLOWERING: *14½ inches (37 cm).*
PAIRS OF LEAVES ON FLOWERING STEM: *8.*
WIDTH AT FIRST FLOWERING: *16 inches (41 cm).*
AROMA AND TASTE: *The small leaves have a perfume of cinnamon, spice, citrus, mint and a tea-like quality. They contain a good, well-rounded taste that is slightly hot with mint, citrus, flowers, spice and just a touch of anise.*

SPICY GLOBE.

SPICY GLOBE. *Ocimum* 'Spicy Globe' (*O. basilicum* × *O. americanum*). In the early 1980s, neighbors of a Northrup King salesman returned from a vacation in Italy with basil seed. When the salesman saw the plant it produced, he took seeds back to the office. By 1985, Northrup King had turned the vacation seed find into a new introduction called 'Spicy Globe'.

'Spicy Globe' is a freely branching, compact plant with a pleasantly rounded shape, suitable for use as a fragrant annual border hedge. Its short stature and vigorous branching create a dense interior that can become a disease vector in humid climates; a bark mulch may restrain disease. The green leaves are subtly veined, with delicately toothed margins; average size is 3/4 inch (2 cm) long by 3/8 inch (1 cm) wide. So compact is the inflorescence that its white flowers open while buried in foliage; eventually the handsome flower spikes elongate to about 3 inches (7.5 cm).

NORMALLY REPRODUCED FROM SEED.
TIMING: *At 70°F (21°C), germination is 3 days; transplant 15 days after sowing; garden ready 32 days after sowing.*
FIRST FLOWERING: *60 days from sowing.*
HEIGHT AT FIRST FLOWERING: *10 inches (25 cm).*
PAIRS OF LEAVES ON FLOWERING STEM: *7.*
WIDTH AT FIRST FLOWERING: *14 inches (36 cm).*

AROMA AND TASTE: *'Spicy Globe' lives up to its name; its strong spicy aroma holds a hint of citrus and mint. The flavor is pungent with spice and mint, slightly hot, with an odd perfumed sensation. The scent derives from a number of chemicals, primarily the floral linalool and the spicy β-caryophyllene.*

SWEET BASIL.

SWEET BASIL. 'Sweet Basil' is one of those catchall terms that is giving way to named varieties which provide consistency from year to year.

On any present 'Sweet Basil', expect green leaves that are smooth or slightly puckered, strongly veined with toothed margins, about 3¼ inches (8 cm) long and 1½ inches (4 cm) wide. Flower stems up to 6 inches (15 cm) long will be filled with white flowers.

NORMALLY REPRODUCED FROM SEED.
TIMING: *At 70°F (21°C), germination is 3 days; transplant 14 days after sowing; garden ready 28 days after sowing.*
FIRST FLOWERING: *55 days from sowing.*
HEIGHT AT FIRST FLOWERING: *23 to 26 inches (58 to 66 cm).*
PAIRS OF LEAVES ON FLOWERING STEM: *7 to 8.*

WIDTH AT FIRST FLOWERING: *12 to 15 inches (30 to 38 cm).*
AROMA AND TASTE: *Sweet basils offer a balanced fragrance of mint, spice, hyacinth, citrus, and anise. Mint and spice greet the tongue first, with some anise, followed by a green herbal taste and a slight pungency. As a group, sweet basils depend on the floral-scented linalool, clove-scented eugenols, and anise-scented methyl chavicol for the high points of their essential oils.*

SWEET FINE.

SWEET FINE. *Ocimum americanum* 'Sweet Fine'. This basil is often associated with France. It grows rather tall and rangy and has small green leaves. In our trials, 'Sweet Fine' reached nearly 3 feet (91 cm) high in a little over two months from sowing, producing long stems with widely spaced leaves. Leaves are medium to dark green, 3/4 to 1¼ inches (2 to 3 cm) long and 3/8 to 3/4 inches (1 to 2 cm) wide, and have margins almost smooth with light veining. White flowers open on loosely branched inflorescences.

NORMALLY REPRODUCED FROM SEED.

TIMING: *At 70°F (21°C), germination is 3 days; transplant 12 days after sowing; garden ready 24 days after sowing.*

FIRST FLOWERING: *69 days from sowing.*

HEIGHT AT FIRST FLOWERING: *24 to 36 inches (61 to 91 cm).*

PAIRS OF LEAVES ON FLOWERING STEM: *8 to 14.*

WIDTH AT FIRST FLOWERING: *16 to 18 inches (41 to 46 cm).*

AROMA AND TASTE: *The basil scent comes through with a balance of spice, mint, citrus, some anise, and an overall sweetness. The taste is pungent and slightly hot with citrus zest, mint, and a hint of musk. The essential oil is dominated by the floral-scented linalool with some spicy notes from β-caryophyllene.*

THAI PURPLE.

THAI PURPLE. *Ocimum basilicum* 'Thai Purple'. A purple-leaved Thai basil has been elusive in the American seed trade, but it is everywhere in Thai restaurants. Tom stumbled across this cultivar by chance in 1995. It appeared among seedlings of 'New Guinea' basil as a few atypical plants and was later identified by several Thai women who saw it in his greenhouse.

Long pointed green leaves 3 inches (7.5 cm) long by 1½ inches (4 cm) wide are heavily mottled with purple; undersides are often all purple. Leaves have delicately toothed margins with some puckering of the surface. Stems are tinged purple, becoming a dark purple toward the terminal. Light violet blossoms with striped violet throats burst from dark purple calyxes; single flower stems are 5½ to 7 inches (14 to 18 cm) long.

NORMALLY REPRODUCED FROM SEED.

TIMING: *At 70°F (21°C), germination is 3 days; transplant 17 days after sowing; garden ready 32 days after sowing.*

FIRST FLOWERING: *51 days from sowing.*

HEIGHT AT FIRST FLOWERING: *18 inches (46 cm).*

PAIRS OF LEAVES ON FLOWERING STEM: *6.*

WIDTH AT FIRST FLOWERING: *12 inches (30 cm).*

AROMA AND TASTE: *The aroma and taste are of anise with floral notes. The scent derives from large amounts of anise-scented methyl chavicol in the essential oil.*

TRUE THAI. *Ocimum basilicum* 'True Thai'. Basil grows wild in Thailand, a habit that can cause confusion when the word "true" is used to delineate a single variety. This introduction from Shepherd's pairs a fine anise flavor with an exquisitely ornamental plant.

'True Thai' has a radiant purple, cone-headed inflorescence filled with many individual stems ringed by six light lavender or pink blossoms. The cone is 3½ inches (9 cm) wide and 3½ inches (9 cm) high, stretching in height as it ages. The plants themselves tend to have flattened tops that match the unique flower formations. Purple suffuses several inches (5 to 8 cm) of the stem tips, as well as the calyxes and bracts. Leaves are similar to other Thai basils in the trade, dark green, generally flat and pointed with margins prominently serrated; typical leaves are 2¼ to 3½ inches (6 to 9 cm) long and 1⅛ to 1¼ inches (3 to 3.2 cm) wide.

NORMALLY REPRODUCED FROM SEED.

TIMING: *At 70°F (21°C), germination is 3 days; transplant 13 days after sowing; garden ready 26 days after sowing.*

FIRST FLOWERING: *63 days from sowing.*

HEIGHT AT FIRST FLOWERING: *19 inches (48 cm).*

PAIRS OF LEAVES ON FLOWERING STEM: *8.*

WIDTH AT FIRST FLOWERING: *20 inches (51 cm).*

AROMA AND TASTE: *'True Thai' has a good, rounded aroma: nice spice, sweet with mint and licorice. Its perfumed flavor is assertive with sweet licorice, then mint and spice. The essential oil is almost pure anise-scented methyl chavicol.*

WEST AFRICAN. *Ocimum gratissimum.* 'West African'. This basil originated in Ghana and was introduced by Richters in 1995. Similar to East Indian basil in appearance but much shorter, it is used in Africa as a medicinal plant to treat fevers and diarrhea, and to repel insects.

'West African' is a short, woody-stemmed plant. The heavy veining of the green leaves give the surface a checkerboard pattern. Leaves are 4½ inches (11 cm) long and 2½ inches (6 cm) wide. Tiny white flowers with yellow-tipped sepals hardly emerge from green calyxes; they are carried in whorls on terminal tips as long as 9 inches (23 cm). The plant can be expected to reach 30 to 40 inches (76 to 102 cm) high and 24 inches (61 cm) wide.

NORMALLY REPRODUCED FROM CUTTINGS.

HEIGHT AT FIRST FLOWERING: *19 inches (48 cm).*

WIDTH AT FIRST FLOWERING: *16 inches (41 cm).*

AROMA AND TASTE: *Leaves give off a musky odor that contains camphor, savory, spice, and a hint of mint. The taste is pungent, resinous, and bitter, qualities that keep this basil out of the kitchen. The scent derives from pine-scented bornyl acetate and the clove-scented methyl eugenol.*

The Recipes

Twenty-five years ago I encountered basil for the first time at an outdoor café in the romantic hills of Tuscany. Tables with white cloths, votive candles flickering in the summer evening breeze, local chianti from a *fiasco*, laughter and camaraderie with Italian friends, all combined to make the perfect setting for a love affair. And mine began with my first bite of *trenette al pesto*. That taste was one of surprise, delight, and intrigue. I was an instant devotee.

No preparation better displays basil's attributes than pesto, and I was so enchanted with the herb after that first night that I *had* to learn how to make it. I knew pesto's ingredients were basil, olive oil, garlic, parmesan, and pine nuts, but I had no recipes and no skills. I found the perfect teacher in Alberto, a young, enthusiastic Italian farmer with an aristocratic background. Born and raised in Tuscany, he made pesto as his mother had taught him.

For my first pesto-making lesson, Alberto took me to his garden to gather basil and flat-leaved parsley. We took the ingredients into the kitchen, where we started a pot of water to boil for the pasta while we washed and dried the herbs. We pulled the leaves from their stems, grated *pecorino romano* (which is the preferred cheese for pesto in that region), and peeled garlic. With the preparations completed, Alberto placed a handful of *pignolia* (pine nuts) and the garlic cloves in a large mortar and began pounding them with the pestle. He pounded the nuts and garlic into a rough paste, and added a handful of basil and parsley. Once the pesto started turning green, he added more herbs, then a little olive oil, and then more herbs. We took turns using the pestle—a labor-intensive job, but the reward is in the end result. Alberto intuitively sensed the right amount of herbs to add, the precise amount of olive oil necessary for the perfect emulsion, and exactly how much cheese should be worked in to obtain the right consistency and balance of flavor. We spooned the just-made pesto over al dente pasta. I was amazed again at the way I reacted to the magic mixture of simple, aromatic ingredients. In Italy, I was awakened to *depth of flavor* for the first time in my life and it changed forever my way of thinking about taste and food.

Since my first Italian encounters, I have made pesto more times and more ways than I can count. Pesto is a subject that can incite, or better yet, ignite, the passion of many an Italian. The first preparation I learned was Tuscan and parsley was a-matter-of-fact ingredient; however, parsley in pesto is unheard of in Southern Italy. Southern Italians sometimes use walnuts in place of pine nuts, but that causes shudders in other parts of the country. In the north, cream is sometimes added to pesto, a matter of great angst to a Sicilian. There are as many versions of pesto as there are regions in Italy, and even more valiant defenders of each version. For my own favorite, refer to the recipe on page 130; for more information on the history of pesto, see page 20.

Many cuisines depend on basil. Italians, Japanese, Chinese, Thais, Vietnamese, French, Americans, and many others use basil just for flavoring noodles. All around the world, recipes both old and new use the aromatic leaves with fresh and cooked vegetables, in salads, with eggs, meats, and seafood, in soups and breads, with all kinds of cheeses, and for seasoning vinegars and oils. Accompanied by fresh tomato slices, basil is wonderful on a sandwich in place of lettuce. It adds a pleasant flavor to butter, vinaigrettes, marinades, and sauces.

Fresh basil should be cooked only briefly or added as a garnish to long-simmered dishes. On occasion, I like to cut the herb leaves crosswise, into fine shreds (chiffonade), rather than always chopping them; chiffonade has a nice texture and looks attractive. In most cases, using a little more or less fresh basil will not make much difference to a dish.

However, you do need to be careful when substituting dried basil in a recipe that calls for fresh. In some cases, dried basil just won't work; as in pesto, the fresh herb is essential. When substituting dried herb for fresh, the ratio is about 1 to 3 to compensate for moisture loss; for example, in a tomato sauce that calls for 3 tablespoons (45 ml) of fresh basil, you would use 1 tablespoon (15 ml) of dried basil. It is always better to season lightly, taste, and then add more if needed. Always try to purchase or dry your basil leaves whole, then crumble them into your preparation as needed. Once crushed, dried leaves lose their essential oils and fragrance quickly; thus, they are not so pungent when stored.

When a recipe calls for sprigs of basil, it always means the fresh herb. Leaves should be removed from the stems unless the recipe directs otherwise. Basil sprigs can be as short as 2 to 3 inches (5 to 8 cm) or as long as 10 to 12 inches (25 to 30 cm). Sprig size depends on the type of plant and its state of maturity.

If a recipe calls for 1 cup (240 ml) packed basil leaves, chopped, you should measure the leaves first and chop them afterwards. When the ingredients call for 1 cup (240 ml) packed coarsely-chopped basil leaves, you should coarsely chop a pile of basil leaves and then measure them, pressing them down in the measuring cup to pack them. Likewise, if the recipe calls for 2 tablespoons (30 ml) chopped basil, chop the leaves first and then measure them. For information on how to dry and preserve fresh basil, see page 50. Some recipes specify the use of non-reactive cookware. If you cook a cream or acidic sauce such as tomato in a reactive pot— iron, aluminum, or copper—the sauce could discolor.   —S.B.

Cheese Torta with Basil,
Olives, and Sundried Tomatoes
is great for entertaining.

Appetizers, Soups, and Breads

Bruschetta with Basil Antipasto

Creamy Summer Tomato and Vegetable Soup

Provençal-Style Vegetable Soup with Pistou

Flatbread Pizzas with Marinated Grilled Vegetables and Basil

Cheese Torta with Basil, Olives, and Sundried Tomatoes

Basil and Cheddar Biscuits

Fig and Basil Muffins

■ Bruschetta with Basil Antipasto

The choice for this preparation is 'Genoa Green' or a sweet green basil. The tomatoes should be peak of the season and summer ripe. The bread should be a crusty, country-style loaf made simply with flour, yeast, water, salt, and a little oil. The bruschetta can be served as a hearty appetizer or first course, or as a main dish for lunch. If you want a smaller, more formal appetizer, serve the basil antipasto on round toasts made from sliced baguettes.

MAKES 12 PORTIONS

1/2 pound (225 g) fresh mozzarella, torn into bite-sized pieces
2 medium tomatoes (about 12 ounces [340 ml]), cut into dice
1 cup (240 ml) Vidalia or other sweet onion, thinly sliced and cut into 1/2-inch
  (1-cm) lengths
Salt and freshly ground pepper
About 3 tablespoons (45 ml) extra-virgin olive oil
Generous 1 cup (240 ml) packed basil leaves, cut crosswise into thin shreds
12 slices bread roughly 3 by 4 inches (8 by 10 cm)
3 or 4 large cloves garlic, peeled

Toss the mozzarella, tomatoes, and onion together in a mixing bowl. Generously salt and pepper, add 2 tablespoons (15 ml) of the oil, the basil, and toss well. Taste for seasoning.

Toast the bread until golden brown on both sides. Rub the toast firmly with the garlic and drizzle lightly with the remaining oil; use a little more oil if necessary. Evenly distribute the basil antipasto over the bruschetta and serve immediately.

■ Creamy Summer Tomato and Vegetable Soup

'Aussie Sweetie', 'Lesbos', or a sweet green basil mixed with a little 'Cinnamon' basil are good in this soup. It's pretty, simple, and quite tasty; it can be served hot or cold, and is good made in advance. We think of this as a summer or harvest-time soup when the tomatoes and basil are at their peak, but it can easily be made in the fall and winter. It won't have as fresh a flavor, but it is still quite tasty. Substitute a 15-ounce (425-g) can of tomatoes, drained, for the ripe ones, and if you don't have fresh basil, use about 2 tablespoons (30 ml) of dried leaves, crumbled coarsely, or a little more to taste.

SERVES 4

2 tablespoons (30 ml) extra-virgin olive oil
1 heaping cup (240 ml) diced red onion
1/2 pound (225 g) potatoes, peeled and diced
2 medium carrots, sliced
1 pound (450 ml) red ripe tomatoes, peeled, seeded, and diced
1 red bell pepper, roasted, peeled, seeded, and diced
Salt and freshly ground pepper
2 cups (475 ml) vegetable or chicken stock
1 cup (240 ml) basil leaves, chopped
2 cups (475 ml) milk
Basil for garnish

Heat the oil in a nonreactive soup pot over medium heat. Sauté the onions for 5 minutes, stirring occasionally. Add the potatoes and carrots, stir, cover and sweat them for 5 minutes. Add the tomatoes and bell pepper, season with salt and pepper, and cook for 3 minutes, stirring occasionally.

Add the stock and cook for about 5 minutes. Add the basil, cover, and let sit for a few minutes.

Puree the soup in batches, in a blender or food processor; return the soup to the pot. Add the milk, stir and heat until the soup just barely simmers. Taste for salt and pepper. Serve hot garnished with basil shreds or whole small leaves.

> You can always perk up canned tomato soup with basil. One of my quick and easy "comfort foods", I've prepared it for the past twenty years or more by adding a clove of fresh garlic, pressed through a garlic press, crumbling in a few dried basil leaves or adding fresh-chopped basil if available, followed by a generous pinch of cayenne pepper. I then cook it for a few minutes, just until it's heated through.

■ Provençal-Style Vegetable Soup with Pistou

This recipe is the French version of minestrone with pesto. Pistou has more cheese and garlic and less basil than pesto and contains chopped tomato or tomato paste. There are as many versions of pistou as there are pesto; all are tasty and reminiscent of the sun-drenched Mediterranean cuisine. This soup was inspired by Julia Child's Soupeau Pistou *from* The Way to Cook.

SERVES 8

2 cups (475 ml) cooked white beans
2 cups (475 ml) bean, vegetable stock, or water
About 1 teaspoon (5 ml) salt
About 4 cups (950 ml) water
1 bay leaf
Generous 1/2 teaspoon (2 ml) thyme
2 stalks celery, sliced crosswise 3/8 inch (8 mm) thick; about 1 cup (240 ml)
2 carrots, sliced crosswise 1/4 inch (5 mm) thick; about 1 cup (240 ml)
3 large leeks, cleaned, trimmed, halved lengthwise, and sliced crosswise 1/4 inch
    (5 mm) thick; about 2$^{1}/_{2}$ cups (590 ml)
1 medium-large potato, cut into dice; about 1$^{1}/_{2}$ cups (360 ml)
1 pound (450 g) tomatoes, peeled and diced or one 15-ounce (425-g) can of
    chopped tomatoes
4 cloves garlic, minced
1 small zucchini, sliced crosswise 1/4 inch (5 mm) thick; about 1 cup (240 ml)
About 12 ounces (340 g) green beans, topped and tailed and cut into 1-inch (2-cm)
    lengths; 2 cups (475 ml)
Generous 1/2 cup (120 ml) broken vermicelli or thin spaghetti, in 1-inch (2-cm) lengths

In a large, nonreactive soup pot combine the beans, stock, salt, and 4 cups (950 ml) water and bring to a simmer. Add the bay leaf, thyme, celery, carrots, leeks, and potatoes and stir. Simmer for 10 minutes, stirring occasionally. Make the pistou while the soup is cooking (recipe follows).

Add the tomatoes and garlic to the soup pot and cook for 5 minutes more. Add the zucchini, green beans, and pasta, stir and cook for 10 minutes more. Taste the soup for seasoning; if the soup seems too thick add a little more water.

The soup can be served immediately, or it can be removed from the heat and gently reheated when ready to serve. Remove the bay leaf before serving. Ladle the hot soup into warmed soup bowls and garnish with a generous spoonful of pistou.

■ Pistou

Adjustments need to be made depending on the variables; how big your tomato is, how fresh the basil is, and how big your garlic cloves are. Taste and add a little more cheese if the flavor is too sharp, or a little more oil if the pistou is too thick—it should be about the consistency of pesto (page 130). The tomato doesn't have to be roasted, but it has better flavor if it is.

MAKES ABOUT 1 CUP (240 ML)

4 large cloves garlic
About 1/4 teaspoon (1 ml) salt
Generous 1/2 cup (120 ml) packed basil leaves, chopped
1 ripe tomato, roasted, peeled, seeded, and finely diced
About 1/3 cup (80 ml) freshly grated parmesan
About 1/3 cup (80 ml) extra-virgin olive oil

Combine the garlic and salt in a large mortar and crush them with the pestle into a smooth paste. Add half the basil to the mortar, crushing the leaves against the sides with the pestle, repeat with the remaining basil. The mixture will be like a coarse, thick paste until the oil is added.

Add the tomato and work with the pestle until it is mashed into the basil and garlic. Stir in the cheese. Drizzle the olive oil in slowly, a bit at a time as you work it in. The pistou should become very smooth and there should not be any big pieces. Once most of the oil is added, taste for seasoning and adjust with a little more oil, cheese, or salt.

If you are using a food processor, combine the garlic, salt, basil, and a few tablespoons of the oil. Process until mixed. Add the tomato and cheese and process until blended. Drizzle in the remaining oil and process until smooth and homogenous. Taste for seasoning, and add a little more oil, cheese, or salt, if desired. If you make it in advance, cover the pistou and let stand at room temperature.

■ Flatbread Pizzas with Marinated Grilled Vegetables and Basil

Grilling vegetables brings out their best flavor. Many vegetables are good on the grill; choose those you like the best or what's in season. Cooking time will vary depending on how hot your grill or broiler are, and how far the vegetables are from the heat. Once the vegetables are prepared and marinated, the rest of the dish is fairly easy to do.

For this recipe, use the Italian-style flatbread shells available in the grocery, the ones that just need to be heated for 5 to 10 minutes. Pita bread or homemade pizza crusts could easily be substituted. Serve the pizzas as a main course with a salad for lunch or supper, or cut them into wedges and serve as hors d'œuvres to a crowd.

SERVES 6 AS A MAIN COURSE, 12 FOR HORS D'ŒUVRES

5- to 6-ounce (140- to 170-g) green zucchini, sliced 1/4 inch (5 mm) thick
5- to 6-ounce (140- to 170-g) yellow squash, sliced 1/4 inch (5 mm) thick
10-ounce (280-g) eggplant, quartered lengthwise and sliced 3/8 inch (8 mm) thick
1 small red bell pepper, stemmed, seeded, and cut lengthwise into 3/4-inch (2-cm) strips
1 cup (240 ml) packed, coarsely-chopped basil leaves
1/4 cup (60 ml) and 3 tablespoons (45 ml) extra-virgin olive oil
2 tablespoons (30 ml) tamari soy sauce
2 tablespoons (30 ml) red wine vinegar
1 tablespoon (15 ml) balsamic vinegar
1/4 cup (60 ml) water
4 cloves garlic, minced or pressed
Salt and freshly ground pepper
1 large Vidalia onion, sliced crosswise about 1/2 inch (1 cm) thick
6 6-inch (15-cm) flatbread shells
Generous 1 cup (240 ml) basil leaves, cut crosswise into thin strips
Freshly grated parmesan cheese

In a large, shallow dish, toss the squash, eggplant, and bell pepper with the coarsely chopped basil leaves.

In a small bowl, combine 1/4 cup (60 ml) olive oil, soy sauce, vinegars, water, and 2 cloves of the garlic. Add salt and pepper to taste and stir well. Pour this marinade over the vegetables. Let the vegetables marinate for at least 1 hour, and up to 3 hours, stirring occasionally.

Add the remaining 2 cloves of garlic to the 3 tablespoons (45 ml) of olive oil.

Prepare a medium-hot wood charcoal fire in a grill and place the rack about 6 inches (15 cm) from the heat. Brush the onion slices with the marinade and grill them on both sides until golden brown, about 4 or 5 minutes on each side. Remove the onions to a baking sheet. Remove the vegetables from the marinade and grill them, turning once, until they are golden brown on both sides. Remove the grilled vegetables to the baking sheet with the onions. Separate the onion rings or cut the slices in half. Salt and pepper the vegetables lightly.

Heat the flatbreads on the grill, top side down, for 3 to 5 minutes. Turn them, so that they are on their bottoms, and brush the tops with the oil and garlic. Grill them until they are hot throughout.

Scatter basil strips over the heated flatbreads and generously arrange grilled vegetables over each bread. Scatter a few more basil strips on top of the vegetables for garnish and sprinkle with parmesan. Serve immediately.

∎ Cheese Torta with Basil, Olives, and Sundried Tomatoes

Because this dish can be prepared in advance, it is a good choice for entertaining. Savory cheese torta makes an attractive presentation surrounded with slices of crusty baguettes or your favorite cracker. It is possible to make this torta with cream cheese only, or with half goat cheese or mild feta and half cream cheese, but the flavor isn't so complex or the taste so rich. 'Genoa Green' basil or one of the small-leaved varieties would work well here. During the holidays, Jennifer Evans improvised on this recipe by making it in the shape of a Christmas tree, covering it with the basil layer, and garnishing it with strips of sundried tomato and olive slices.

SERVES 6 TO 8

Large basil leaves
About 10 ounces (280 g) goat cheese, softened
8 ounces (225 g) cream cheese, softened
1/4 to 1/2 cup (60 to 120 ml) milk
3 cloves garlic, minced
Salt and freshly ground pepper
Generous 1/2 cup (120 ml) finely chopped basil leaves
About 1 tablespoon (15 ml) extra-virgin olive oil
1/2 cup (120 ml) finely chopped sundried tomatoes packed in oil, drained
1/2 cup (120 ml) finely chopped Kalamata olives

Use a 1-quart (1-liter) domed bowl (not flat like a soup bowl) and a piece of dampened cheesecloth to line the bowl. Arrange some basil leaves, face side down on the cheesecloth.

In another bowl, mix the goat cheese and cream cheese together and add enough milk so that the mixture is smooth and fairly easy to spread. Add one clove of the minced garlic, season with salt and pepper, and mix well. In a third bowl, combine the rest of the basil with the remaining garlic and add olive oil to make a thick paste.

Spread one-fourth of the cheese carefully over the basil leaves in the bottom of the domed bowl. Evenly add the sundried tomatoes, spreading them to the edge of the cheese, and press down gently. Spread one-fourth of the cheese over the tomatoes. Spread the basil and garlic over this layer, pressing lightly. Add a third layer of cheese, and cover it with the olives, spreading them evenly to the edge and pressing gently. Finish with the remaining layer of cheese, cover this with whole, large basil leaves and press down gently. Fold the cheesecloth in to cover the cheese torta and refrigerate at least 2 hours before serving.

To serve, fold back the cheesecloth and turn it out onto a serving plate. Carefully remove the cheesecloth from what is now the top of the torta. Let the torta stand at room temperature for 10 to 15 minutes before serving.

■ Basil and Cheddar Biscuits

The tomato paste in this dough results in biscuits that are tinged orange-pink and flecked with green. The flavor is a winning combination—tomatoes, basil, cheddar, and a hint of garlic—rich and savory. No butter needed! If you want to make these during cold weather and you have no fresh basil, use about 1$^1/_2$ tablespoons (22 ml) of dried basil. Crumble the dried leaves into the milk. These biscuits won't have the same perfume and taste as the ones prepared with fresh basil, but they are still quite nice.

ABOUT 2 DOZEN BISCUITS

2 cups less 2 tablespoons (445 ml) unbleached flour
1/2 cup (120 ml) whole wheat flour
1/2 teaspoon (2 ml) salt
2 teaspoons (10 ml) baking powder
6 tablespoons (90 ml) unsalted butter
1 cup (240 ml) 2% or whole milk
2 tablespoons (30 ml) tomato paste
1 large clove garlic
2/3 cup (160 ml) finely grated sharp cheddar cheese
1/2 cup (120 ml) finely minced basil

Preheat the oven to 400°F (200°C). Combine the flours, salt, and baking powder in a large bowl and blend thoroughly. Cut in the butter until the mixture resembles a coarse meal.

In a small bowl, combine the milk with the tomato paste, blending well. Press the garlic through a garlic press into the milk and stir. Add the liquid to the dry ingredients along with the cheese and basil, and stir to form a soft dough.

Turn the dough onto a floured pastry marble or board, knead gently until it just comes together, and roll out to 1/2-inch (1-cm) thickness. Cut the dough into 1$^3/_4$- to 2-inch (4.5- to 5-cm) squares, diamonds, or rounds and place on an ungreased baking sheet.

Bake the biscuits for 15 to 18 minutes or until light golden brown. Remove to a baking rack to cool slightly before serving. The biscuits are best served warm and right after baking. If you want to prepare them in advance, cool them completely and store them in an air-tight container. Wrap them in foil and gently reheat in a 325°F (160°C) oven for 10 to 15 minutes.

■ Fig and Basil Muffins

These golden, toothsome little muffins are full of unusual flavors—the honey and figs give sweetness, the basil lends a lovely perfume, and the olive oil and cornmeal provide a delicious wholesome taste. Use whichever fig you prefer; I've made these with both golden calymyra and black mission, and the latter is my favorite. If the figs are really dry, soak them in warm water for 15 minutes or so, and pat them dry. As for basils, 'Genoa Green', 'Aussie Sweetie', 'Spicy Bush', or even 'Cinnamon' are good choices.

MAKES 12 MUFFINS

1¹/₂ cups (360 ml) unbleached flour
1 cup (240 ml) stone-ground yellow cornmeal
1/2 teaspoon (2 ml) salt
2 teaspoons (10 ml) baking powder
1 cup (240 ml) chopped figs
1 extra-large egg
1¹/₃ cups (320 ml) milk
1/4 cup (60 ml) olive oil
1/4 cup (60 ml) mild-flavored honey
1 cup basil leaves, coarsely chopped

Preheat oven to 400°F (200°C). Line muffin pan with paper liners or generously butter a muffin pan.

Mix the flour, cornmeal, salt, and baking powder in a bowl. Toss the figs into the dry ingredients. Make a well in the dry ingredients.

In a small bowl, beat the egg lightly. Add the milk, oil, and honey and blend well. Stir in the basil, and pour the liquid ingredients into the dry; stir until just mixed.

Fill the muffin cups almost to the rim. Bake in a hot oven for 20 to 22 minutes, until the muffins are golden brown. Allow the muffins to cool a few minutes before serving. They are best served when warm. If you want to reheat the muffins, wrap them in foil and heat them at 300°F (150°C) for about 15 minutes.

Polenta with 'Anise' Basil
Tomato Sauce

Pasta and Main Dishes

Egg Pasta with Basil Leaves

Pasta with Summer Tomatoes and Basil

Winter Pasta with Quick Tomato Basil Sauce

Savory Bread Pudding

Thai-Style Noodles with Peanut Basil Sauce

Polenta with 'Anise' Basil Tomato Sauce

■ Egg Pasta with Basil Leaves

This pasta can be prepared in many ways—with the green leaves showing through the yellow egg pasta, it deserves to be shown off. Use it in lasagna or cannelloni, or cut it into pappardelle shapes and serve it with a simple sauce of good olive oil and garlic, maybe a little balsamic vinegar, and pass the parmesan. In a light vegetable or chicken broth, it also serves as a good first course.

THIS RECIPE MAKES TWO BATCHES OF PASTA, OR ABOUT 2/3 POUND (300 G), ENOUGH FOR 4 MAIN-COURSE OR 6 APPETIZER SERVINGS.

2 cups (475 ml) unbleached flour
2 extra-large eggs
About 1 cup (240 ml) small whole basil leaves with stem ends removed

Heap the flour and make a well in it. Break the eggs into the well and beat them together with a fork. Stir the eggs into the flour from the bottom of the well with a fork until the dough in the center is smooth and shiny. Using your hands, incorporate the flour from the outside under the center, kneading gently until the mass of dough is consistent but still soft.

Knead the flour into the dough until the dough is smooth and resilient. You probably will not incorporate all of the flour. If the dough is sticky, or very pliable, keep kneading flour into it. Divide the dough into two portions and cover it with plastic wrap or an overturned bowl. Let it rest for at least 30 minutes before putting it through a pasta machine.

To make the dough in a food processor, put the flour in the work bowl with the steel blade and pulse. Add the eggs and process about 30 seconds. The dough should just turn over itself at the top of the bowl. Test by stopping the machine and pinching a bit of the dough together. If it coheres readily, turn it out and knead it. If not, add water, a teaspoonful at a time, and process. Be careful not to add too much water.

Processor dough is stiffer than hand-worked dough. Divide into two portions, cover, and let rest for at least 30 minutes before rolling.

When the dough is rested, begin rolling one portion through the machine at the widest setting of the rollers. Fold it in thirds, and run it through the widest setting another time or two. Always put an unfolded side into the machine when adding folded dough. If the dough feels wet or sticky, dust it lightly with flour before you roll it through the machine.

Advance the rollers and put the dough through the machine without folding. Roll the dough through the first two or three settings of the pasta machine, until it is about 1/8 inch (3 mm) thick.

Cut the length of rolled pasta in half and cover one piece with whole basil leaves laid closely together. Carefully lay the other piece of the pasta over the leaves and press gently yet firmly with the heels of your hands to sandwich the leaves between the pasta.

Set the pasta machine back one notch from the last setting used (usually the next-to-the-last setting) and roll this pasta through the machine until it is 1/16 inch (1.5 mm) thick.

Lay the pasta on a lightly floured surface and cut it with a pasta cutter into pappardelle (1½- to 2-inch [4- to 5-cm] squares or rectangles), or shape as desired. Repeat the rolling and cutting process with the other portion of dough.

At this point the pasta can be spread on baking sheets and left to dry a bit or covered with plastic wrap and refrigerated until ready to use; it is best used fresh. Cooking time will vary depending on how fresh the pasta is, but it should be served al dente. Cook it in gently boiling well-salted water, and have its broth hot, or its sauce prepared.

■ Pasta with Summer Tomatoes and Basil

The great thing about this recipe is that you can prepare the whole thing in the time it takes to boil the water and cook the pasta—a quick, delicious summer dish you can count on. You can also use 1 pound (240 ml) of unfilled, dried pasta such as ziti, shells, or bow ties; the dish won't be quite as substantial as with the filled pasta. As for basil, 'Genoa Green', a sweet green, a bush basil, or a combination of the three is good here.

SERVES 6

About 2 tablespoons (30 ml) extra-virgin olive oil

1 cup (240 ml) diced sweet onion such as Vidalia or Walla Walla

3 large, summer-ripe tomatoes, cored and diced

2 to 3 cloves garlic, finely minced

Salt and freshly ground black pepper

2/3 cup (160 ml) chopped fresh basil leaves

About 18 ounces (510 g) fresh cheese ravioli or tortelloni

Freshly grated parmesan

Basil leaves for garnish

Bring a large, nonreactive pot of water to boil for cooking the pasta.

In a large skillet, heat the oil over medium heat. Add the onion, stir, and sauté for about 6 minutes. Add the tomatoes and garlic and season with salt and pepper; stir and cover.

Reduce heat to medium low and cook for 5 minutes. Add the basil, stir, cover and cook for 1 minute. Remove from heat.

Cook the pasta until it is al dente. Drain, saving about 1/4 cup (60 ml) of the cooking water. Add the pasta and water to the sauce and toss well. Taste for seasoning, add a bit more olive oil if necessary, and serve hot. Garnish with parmesan and basil leaves.

■ Winter Pasta with Quick Tomato Basil Sauce

In the cold weather of winter, when summer-ripe tomatoes are gone and bunches of fragrant basil may be only a dream, you can make this dish using your home-dried basil or basil packed in oil. This recipe came about one day when the pantry was virtually bare and I wanted more than a sandwich for lunch. Easy and quick like summer pasta, the dish can be prepared in the time it takes to boil the water and cook the pasta. The robust sauce is very thick and concentrated, but it's packed with flavor and coats the pasta well. Olives are optional, although they add a tangy contrast to the sweetness of the tomato and basil.

SERVES 4 TO 6

About 2¹/₂ tablespoons (38 ml) just-crumbled dried basil
1/2 cup (120 ml) red wine or water
4 tablespoons (60 ml) extra-virgin olive oil
1 cup (240 ml) chopped red onion
3 large cloves garlic, minced
1 6-ounce (170-g) can tomato paste
1 pound (450 g) dried pasta such as linguini, spaghetti, vermicelli, or capellini
1/3 cup (80 ml) chopped Kalamata olives
Freshly grated parmesan

In a large nonreactive pot, bring water to boil for cooking the pasta. Crumble the dried basil into the red wine.

In a large skillet, heat 3 tablespoons (45 ml) oil over medium heat. Add the onion, stir, and sauté for about 5 minutes. Add the garlic and tomato paste to the onions and stir with the back of a wooden spoon for 1 minute. Add the wine and basil, stirring well to blend with the tomato paste and onions. Cook the sauce over low heat for a few minutes until the pasta is done.

Cook the pasta until it is al dente. Reserve 1/2 cup (120 ml) of the pasta water and add it to the sauce along with the pasta and toss well. Drizzle the pasta with the remaining tablespoon (15 ml) of olive oil, add the olives, toss, and serve hot. Pass the parmesan.

Put the noodles in the boiling water to cook. Stir and cook the sauce for about 5 minutes. Taste the sauce and adjust with sugar, lime juice, soy sauce, and red pepper flakes. Drain the al dente noodles, saving about 1/4 cup (60 ml) of the cooking water to toss with the sauce, and transfer them to a warmed serving bowl. Add the snowpeas, most of the bean sprouts, and about three-quarters of the basil. Pour the sauce over the noodles and vegetables and toss well.

Garnish the dish with the remaining bean sprouts, basil, and chopped peanuts and serve immediately. Pass red pepper flakes, chopped peanuts, and lime wedges in little bowls.

■ Polenta with 'Anise' Basil Tomato Sauce

Polenta is dried Italian corn ground a little finer than grits and cooked like corn meal mush. The first time I ate polenta in Italy, it was served with a tomato sauce that bore a liberal amount of fennel seed. 'Anise' or 'Licorice' basil provides that flavor here. If you don't have either, substitute green basil and 1 teaspoon (5 ml) of bruised fennel seed. Use any mushroom you have on hand; the portabella is nice and meaty. Tom's technique for cooking polenta with a little more flavor is to sauté some cloves of minced garlic in a few tablespoons of olive oil in the bottom of the pot. Then he mixes the dried polenta with cold chicken or beef stock, rather than water, and proceeds with the directions below for cooking the polenta once the water has boiled.

SERVES 4 TO 6

1¹/₂ quarts (1.5 l) water
1¹/₂ teaspoons (8 ml) salt
1¹/₂ cups (360 ml) polenta
About 2 tablespoons (30 ml) extra-virgin olive oil
1¹/₃ cups (320 ml) diced red onion
1 medium stalk celery, halved lengthwise and thinly sliced; about 1/2 cup (120 ml)
1 medium carrot, halved lengthwise and thinly sliced; about 1/2 cup (120 ml)
1 large portabella mushroom, stem removed, halved and cut into slices; about
   1¹/₂ cups (360 ml)
2 cloves garlic, minced
28-ounce (800-g) can crushed or chopped tomatoes or about 2 pounds (900 g)
   fresh tomatoes, peeled and pureed
1 cup (240 ml) 'Anise' or 'Licorice' basil leaves, coarsely chopped
1/2 teaspoon (2 ml) sugar, optional
1/2 cup (120 ml) 'Anise' or 'Licorice' basil leaves, cut crosswise into thin strips
Freshly grated parmesan

Bring the water to a boil in a large nonreactive pot, then add the salt. Slowly stir the polenta into the boiling water in a steady stream, stirring continuously. When the polenta begins to bubble and erupt, reduce the heat to medium low or low; the polenta should continue to cook but not spatter out of the pot. Cook the polenta, stirring regularly so that it doesn't stick, for 35 to 40 minutes. The polenta should be thick.

At this point, the polenta can be served into bowls, topped with sauce, and garnished with basil, or it can be poured into a loaf pan and allowed to cool. Once cooled, the polenta can be refrigerated for up to three days. If you're making the dish with cold polenta, turn it out of the pan and cut it into slices about 5/8 inch (1.5 cm) thick, then into pieces about 2 inches (5 cm) square. Lightly brush the squares with olive oil and place them on a baking sheet under the broiler, on a griddle over medium heat, or on a grill over a medium hot fire.

Depending on your heat source, the polenta should be cooked for 3 to 5 minutes on each side, or until it is turning golden brown on the edges. Arrange the polenta on a platter or serving plates and spoon the sauce on top.

To make the sauce, heat 2 tablespoons (30 ml) olive oil in a nonreactive skillet over medium heat. Add the onion and stir 1 minute. Add the celery and carrot and stir occasionally for 4 minutes. Cover and sweat the vegetables for 4 minutes. Add the mushrooms and garlic, stir and cook for 2 minutes. Add the tomatoes, stir well and cook for about 5 minutes; if using fresh tomatoes, cook for 5 to 10 minutes more.

Taste the sauce and add salt and sugar, if necessary. Add the chopped basil, stir, cover, and remove from heat. Let stand for 5 minutes. Taste for seasoning. Spoon the sauce over the polenta, sprinkle with parmesan, and generously garnish with the basil strips.

Vegetables and Salads

Salad with Purple and Lettuce Leaf Basils

Baked Eggplant Rounds with Tomatoes and Basil

Corn and Roasted Red Pepper Pudding

Favorite Mashed Potatoes

Stewed Tomatoes with 'Cinnamon' Basil

Potato and Green Bean Salad

White Bean and Pasta Salad

Salad with Purple and Lettuce Leaf Basils is colorful and simple, yet delicious.

■ Salad with Purple and Lettuce Leaf Basils

This tasty, bright salad is simple yet delicious. Use a mixture of the choicest greens and both red and yellow tomatoes for the best flavor and vivid color. If you are making the salad in advance, prepare the greens, tomatoes, and vinaigrette, but save the basil for the last moment. Basil leaves tend to turn brown once they have been cut and washed. Serve this salad with thick slices of toasted bread rubbed with garlic and drizzled with olive oil.

SERVES 6 TO 8

About 12 cups (3 l) mixed lettuces and salad greens such as: red or green leaf, Boston,
*   bibb, deer tongue, oak leaf, or limestone lettuces, spinach, chicory, endive, or frisée*
About 3 cups (710 ml) lettuce leaf basil leaves
About 1 cup (240 ml) purple basil leaves
1 pint (475 ml) basket of baby pear tomatoes
About 1/4 cup (60 ml) basil, balsamic, or red wine vinegar
About 1/2 teaspoon (2 ml) salt
About 1 cup extra-virgin olive oil
1 large clove garlic, finely minced
Freshly ground pepper

Wash the salad greens well and spin them dry. Tear the leaves into large pieces, if necessary. Rinse the basil leaves and spin them dry. Wash the tomatoes and halve them lengthwise.

Pour the vinegar into a small bowl, add the salt, and stir well with a fork. Add the oil, garlic, and pepper and stir until blended. Taste for seasoning; stir well before using.

Arrange the greens on a large serving platter. Scatter the basil leaves over the greens. Scatter the tomatoes over the salad. Dress the salad just before serving, or serve the salad and pass the vinaigrette.

■ Baked Eggplant Rounds with Tomatoes and Basil

These rounds are a good way to get your kids to eat eggplant. Rather like little pizzas, they employ eggplant in place of crust. If you have summer-ripe tomatoes, slice them thin and use them for this quick and easy preparation. For an equally tasty dish, leftover tomato sauce can be used when tomatoes aren't in season.

MAKES ABOUT 15 TO 18 SLICES; SERVES 4 TO 6

About 1 to 1¼ pound (450 to 560 g) eggplant, peeled and sliced into 1/2-inch
  (1-cm) thick rounds
2 tablespoons (30 ml) extra-virgin olive oil with 1 clove minced or pressed garlic
Salt and freshly ground pepper
About 18 large basil leaves
2 large tomatoes, cored and cut into 1/4-inch (5-mm) thick slices or about 1 cup
  (240 ml) tomato sauce
About 1½ cups (360 ml) grated part-skim mozzarella
About 1/4 cup (60 ml) shredded basil leaves

Preheat oven to 375°F (190°C). Lightly brush a baking sheet with olive oil. Place the
eggplant slices on the baking sheet and brush them with the garlic oil.
    Roast the slices in a preheated oven for about 12 minutes. Turn, brush with the remain-
ing garlic oil, and roast for 5 minutes more.
    Remove the eggplant slices from the oven and season with salt and pepper. Place a
large basil leaf on top of each slice. Then layer on a slice of tomato seasoned with a little
salt and pepper, or a generous tablespoon (15 ml) of sauce to cover. Evenly sprinkle with
grated mozzarella. Return the slices to the oven and roast for about 8 minutes more.
They're done if the eggplant feels soft when pierced with a fork and the cheese is melted
and just starting to turn golden.
    Remove from the oven. Garnish with the shredded basil and serve immediately.

■   Corn and Roasted Red Pepper Pudding

The combination of corn and red bell pepper complemented by basil is a summertime trio that
can't be beat. Heavily studded with vegetables, this creamy custard can accompany grilled chick-
en or fish, or it can stand as a light main course served with a tomato salad and some crusty
bread.

SERVES 6

1 tablespoon (15 ml) extra-virgin olive oil
1 tablespoon (15 ml) unsalted butter
1 medium onion, diced
2½ cups (590 ml) fresh corn kernels; about 4 large ears
1 large red bell pepper, roasted, peeled, seeded, and diced
1 garlic clove, finely minced

Salt and freshly ground pepper
3 extra-large eggs
1²/₃ cups (400 ml) milk
2 tablespoons (30 ml) unbleached flour
3/4 cup (180 ml) freshly grated parmesan cheese
1/2 cup (120 ml) packed basil leaves, cut into thin shreds

Preheat oven to 375°F (190°C). Butter an oval or round 1½-quart (1.5-l) gratin dish.
Heat the oil and butter in a sauté pan over medium-low heat. Add the onion and sauté about 8 minutes, stirring occasionally. Add the corn and cook 5 minutes more. Stir in the bell pepper and garlic, season lightly with salt and pepper, and sauté 1 minute more.

Beat the eggs in a large bowl. Add the milk and whisk. Whisk in the flour and parmesan and season generously with salt and pepper. Stir the vegetables into the egg and milk mixture and add the basil leaves. Stir and pour the mixture into the prepared dish.

Bake in a preheated oven for about 25 minutes, until the top is golden brown. Let the pudding stand for 5 minutes before cutting into wedges. It is good served hot or at room temperature.

∎ Favorite Mashed Potatoes

Mashed potatoes are a comfort food. Usually served with gravy or stewed tomatoes, in this recipe they stand on their own. My family loves mashed potatoes and there are rarely leftovers. A sweet green basil is the herb of choice here.

SERVES 4

About 2 pounds (900 g) potatoes
2/3 cup (160 ml) milk
3 tablespoons (45 ml) unsalted butter
1 large clove garlic
Salt and freshly ground pepper
1/2 cup (120 ml) finely chopped sweet green basil leaves

Peel the potatoes one at a time, cut into 3/4-inch (2-cm) pieces, and place immediately in a nonreactive pot of cold water. When all the potatoes are cut, drain off the water and cover again with fresh water. Salt the water lightly. Place the pot, covered, over moderately high heat, bring to a boil, and reduce heat to a simmer. Cook the potatoes until they are fork tender, about 10 to 15 minutes.

Meanwhile, combine the milk and butter in a small saucepan. Squeeze the garlic through a press into the mixture and season generously with salt and pepper. Heat the mixture until the milk is hot and the butter is melted, stirring once or twice. Remove the pan from heat and stir the basil into the milk mixture.

Drain the potatoes, leaving just a bit of the cooking liquid. Pour the milk mixture over the hot potatoes in the pot and mash them with a potato masher. Work the milk and the potatoes together with the potato masher until they are creamy. Taste for seasoning and add more salt or pepper if necessary. Serve immediately, or cover the pot with the lid and hold for 10 minutes or so.

If necessary, place the potatoes, covered, in a 250°F (120°C) oven and hold for up to 30 minutes.

■ Stewed Tomatoes with 'Cinnamon' Basil

My grandmother always put a little cinnamon in her stewed tomatoes. I've made this recipe with my grandmother's stewed tomatoes in mind, using 'Cinnamon' basil for extra flavor and perfume. If you don't have 'Cinnamon' basil, use sweet green with a few pinches of cinnamon. These stewed tomatoes are full of flavor and crunchy with vegetables; my family loves them served over mashed or baked potatoes. Make a double batch and serve them later in the week with chicken, meatloaf, or grilled or baked eggplant or zucchini slices.

MAKES 4 TO 6 SERVINGS

1¹/₂ tablespoons (22 ml) olive oil
1 medium onion, diced
1 large stalk celery, diced
1 small red or green bell pepper, diced
3 cloves garlic, minced
2 pounds (900 g) red ripe tomatoes, peeled and chopped or one 28-ounce (800-g)
  can of tomatoes, chopped
1/2 cup (120 ml) water or tomato juice
1/2 teaspoon (2 ml) salt
Freshly ground pepper
1/2 cup (120 ml) chopped 'Cinnamon' basil leaves or 1 tablespoon (15 ml) dried
  'Cinnamon' basil, crumbled
1 teaspoon (5 ml) packed brown sugar
1 teaspoon (5 ml) Hungarian paprika

In a large nonstick skillet, heat the oil over medium heat. Add the onion, celery, and bell pepper and sauté for 5 minutes. Add the garlic, stir and sauté for 1 minute. Add tomatoes, water, salt, and pepper to taste; stir well and cook for 10 minutes. Add basil, brown sugar, and paprika, stir and cook for 10 minutes, at a bare simmer. Taste for seasoning; add a little more water, if necessary. Serve hot. These can be made ahead and reheated.

■ Potato and Green Bean Salad

This is a simple, straightforward recipe for potato salad with basil making the difference in flavor. Use a sweet green basil here—any of the little bush basil leaves can be used, and you can add a little 'Thai', 'Holly's Painted', or a hint of 'Spice' for extra flavor. Surround this salad with red and yellow pear or cherry tomatoes for a tasty accompaniment.

An alternative if you have leftover pesto: prepare the potatoes, beans, and onions as described here and toss them with about 3/4 cup (180 ml) pesto that has been thinned with a little lemon juice, or balsamic or white wine vinegar to taste.

SERVES 8

2 pounds (900 g) red-skinned potatoes

3/4 pound (340 g) green beans, topped, tailed, and halved

About 5 tablespoons (75 ml) extra-virgin olive oil

2 tablespoons (30 ml) fresh lemon juice or balsamic vinegar

1 clove garlic, finely minced

1 tablespoon (15 ml) Dijon-style mustard

Salt and freshly ground black pepper

3/4 cup (180 ml) finely diced red onion

1 generous cup (240 ml) coarsely chopped basil

If using large potatoes, cut them into quarters lengthwise and slice crosswise 1/4 inch (5 mm) thick. For small potatoes, halve them lengthwise and slice 1/4 inch (5 mm) thick.

Cook the potatoes in a nonreactive pan in lightly salted boiling water for 6 to 9 minutes, until they are crisp tender. Do not overcook; they should be cooked, but firm. Refresh briefly under cold water and drain.

Cook the beans in a nonreactive pan in lightly salted boiling water for 3 to 5 minutes, until crisp tender. Refresh briefly under cold water and drain.

While the vegetables are cooking, combine the oil, lemon juice or vinegar, garlic, and mustard in a small bowl. Season with salt and pepper and stir well with a fork.

Combine the warm potatoes and beans in a bowl with the onions and season well with salt and pepper. Pour the vinaigrette over the vegetables, add the basil, and toss well. Taste for seasoning and adjust with salt, pepper, oil, and lemon juice or vinegar, if necessary.

Garnish the salad with fresh basil leaves and serve warm or at room temperature. If prepared in advance and refrigerated, allow to come to cool room temperature before serving.

■ White Bean and Pasta Salad

This pasta salad can be served as an accompaniment to a meal or as a main course with some crusty bread, cheese, olives, and wine. It's even better after it sits awhile. For a vibrant salad, use about one-third cup (80 ml) of purple basil here, along with the green. If you use all purple basil, the taste is not so good, since the green basils have a richer, more rounded flavor.

SERVES 10

1 pound (450 g) dried pasta such as bow ties, fusilli, or cavatappi
About 6 tablespoons (90 ml) extra-virgin olive oil or basil oil
2 large cloves garlic, finely minced
Salt and freshly ground pepper
1 roasted red bell pepper, peeled, seeded, and cut into pieces 1/4 by 1 inch
   (5 mm by 2.5 cm) wide
2 medium tomatoes, diced
About 1 cup (240 ml) chopped Vidalia, Walla Walla, or other sweet onion
About 2 cups (475 ml) cooked cannellini beans or one 15-ounce (425-g) can,
   drained and rinsed
3 to 4 tablespoons (45 to 60 ml) balsamic vinegar
1 packed cup (240 ml) chopped basil leaves
Green and/or purple basil leaves

Cook the pasta in a nonreactive pot in abundant, lightly salted, boiling water until it is al dente. Drain the pasta, transfer it to a large bowl, and toss with 2 tablespoons (30 ml) of the oil and garlic. Season the pasta with salt and pepper and toss.

Add the bell pepper, tomatoes, onion, and beans to the pasta and toss to combine. In a small bowl, combine the remaining oil with 3 tablespoons (45 ml) of the vinegar and stir well with a fork. Pour the vinaigrette over the pasta and vegetables, add the basil and toss well to combine. Taste for salt, pepper, oil, and vinegar, and adjust as necessary.

The pasta is best if allowed to stand for 30 minutes before serving. Toss and taste for seasoning just before serving. Garnish with purple and green basil leaves and serve at room temperature.

Sauces and Condiments

Shallot and Basil Vinaigrette

Basil Vinegar

Tomato, Black Bean, and Corn Salsa

Basil Butter

Basil Mayonnaise

Raspberry and Opal Basil Vinegar

'Lemon' Basil and White Wine Jelly

Buttermilk Dressing with Basil and Sundried Tomatoes

Italian-Style Pesto

Basil Vinegars add zest to all kinds of salads.

■ Shallot and Basil Vinaigrette

Good on green salads of spinach, tender lettuces, bitter greens, arugula, and watercress, this dressing is also tasty on warm potato or bean salad. It serves as a sauce for grilled vegetables or fish. The vinaigrette will keep, tightly covered in a jar, for five days in the refrigerator.

MAKES ABOUT 3/4 CUP (180 ML)

1 large shallot, minced
1/2 cup (120 ml) packed basil leaves, chopped
About 1/2 cup (120 ml) extra-virgin olive oil
About 2 tablespoons (30 ml) balsamic vinegar
1 teaspoon (5 ml) Dijon-style mustard
Salt and freshly ground pepper

Combine the shallot, basil, oil, vinegar, mustard, salt, and pepper in a blender. Blend until smooth. Taste for salt, pepper, oil, and vinegar. Add a bit more oil and vinegar if you prefer a thinner consistency. Remove from the refrigerator about 15 to 20 minutes before serving.

■ Basil Vinegar

All varieties of culinary basil—'Anise', 'Aussie Sweetie', 'Cinnamon', 'Genoa Green', 'Lemon', 'Spicy Globe', and 'Thai'—make good vinegar. Use white wine or rice wine vinegar to allow the flavors of the herbs to come through; distilled is a bit too harsh. One of my favorite basil vinegars was made with the prunings from an assortment of basils that a certain herb grower of our acquaintance was discarding. The strong basil taste is predominant, with hints of lemon, anise, and spice. Be creative and experiment.

MAKES 1 QUART (1 LITER)

2 to 3 cups (475 to 710 ml) packed basil
3 to 4 cups (710 to 950 ml) white wine or rice wine vinegar

Wash the basil and spin or pat it dry. Pick off any dark or wilted leaves. Put the basil into a clean 1-quart (1-l) canning jar; it should fill the jar about two-thirds full. Pour the vinegar into the jar to fill it 1/2 inch (1 cm) from the top. Place a piece of plastic wrap over the top of the jar. Seal the jar and let it stand in a sunny window or in a sunny spot in the herb garden for about 4 weeks. Taste the vinegar after 2 or 3 weeks; if it tastes good to you, it's bottling time. The longer the herb is infused, the stronger the taste.

Pour the vinegar through a strainer lined with a paper towel or a coffee filter. Pour the vinegar into clean bottles, and put an identifying sprig of fresh basil in the liquid. Label the bottles and store the vinegar away from light, in a cool place. Use within one year.

■ Tomato, Black Bean, and Corn Salsa

'Mexican Spice', 'Peruvian', 'Puerto Rican', or 'Spicy Globe' basil add zest to this salsa. If you use canned black beans, rinse them with water in a colander and drain them well. This mixture can be served as a salsa with chips or as a topping for tostadas; as a relish/salad, it may be served with grilled fish, fowl, or pork.

MAKES A GENEROUS QUART (1 LITER)

3 large, ripe tomatoes, about 1¹/₂ pounds (675 g)
1¹/₂ to 2 cups (360 to 475 ml) canned or cooked black beans, drained
1 generous cup (240 ml) fresh corn kernels (about 2 large ears corn)
1 large bunch scallions, thinly sliced
2 garlic cloves, minced
Hot peppers to taste; at least 3, stemmed, seeded, and diced very small
1¹/₂ to 2 tablespoons (22 to 30 ml) fresh lime juice
About 1/2 teaspoon (2 ml) salt
Freshly ground pepper
Generous 1/2 cup (120 ml) chopped basil

Core the tomatoes and cut them into small dice. In a bowl, combine them with the beans, corn, scallions, garlic, and hot peppers and toss well. Sprinkle the lime juice, salt, pepper, and basil over the vegetables and toss well.

Let the salsa stand for about 30 minutes, taste for seasoning, and serve. Adjust with a little more salt, pepper, lime juice, or hot pepper.

■ Basil Butter

Basil butter is easy to make and a good thing to have on hand. Use a combination of basils or a single favorite; add a little lemon zest for a change. The olive oil is not absolutely necessary, but I like its flavor with the basil and garlic. This butter is great on mashed or baked potatoes, tossed with noodles, on any steamed vegetable, or served with warm biscuits or rolls. Place a pat of the butter on broiled or grilled fish or chicken just before serving. It will keep, tightly covered, in the refrigerator for up to a week, and can be frozen for one month.

MAKES A SCANT 1 CUP (240 ML)

1/2 cup (120 ml) unsalted butter, softened
2 tablespoons (30 ml) extra-virgin olive oil
1 garlic clove
2/3 cup (160 ml) packed basil leaves
Salt and freshly ground pepper

Combine the butter, olive oil, and garlic in a food processor and process until almost smooth. Add the herb leaves and pulse until they have been minced and incorporated into the butter. Season with salt and pepper to taste.

Pack the butter in a small crock or bowl, and cover and refrigerate until ready to serve. Remove from the refrigerator and let stand at room temperature for about 10 minutes before serving.

▪ Basil Mayonnaise

The best-textured mayonnaise is made in a mortar and pestle. Making mayonnaise in a food processor using the whole egg, rather than just the yolk, also produces a good result. Basil mayonnaise is a wonderful condiment for any summer vegetable, for salads, or sandwiches. If there is a problem with eggs in your area, do not prepare this recipe.

MAKES ABOUT 1 CUP (240 ML)

1 garlic clove, peeled and thinly sliced
About 1/2 cup (120 ml) packed basil leaves, coarsely chopped
2/3 to 1 cup (160 to 240 ml) olive oil or vegetable oil
1 extra-large egg, separated, at room temperature
1 1/2 to 2 tablespoons (22 to 30 ml) freshly squeezed lemon juice
Salt and freshly ground pepper

Put the garlic in the mortar and pound it to a paste. Chop the basil leaves and pound them in the mortar until they join the paste, adding just a little oil if necessary.

Stir the egg yolk into the basil and garlic mixture, along with about a tablespoon of lemon juice, and a pinch of salt. Begin to add the oil a few drops at a time, stirring constantly. When about 1/4 cup (60 ml) has been added, pour the oil in a fine stream. Continue until the oil has been used and emulsion has formed. Season to taste with salt, pepper, and lemon juice.

To make the mayonnaise in a food processor or blender, use the whole egg or the yolk. Add the sliced garlic and chopped basil to the processor bowl or blender jar. Add the egg or yolk, a little lemon juice, and a pinch of salt. With the motor running, add the oil in a very fine stream, until emulsion has formed. Finish the seasoning with lemon juice, salt, and pepper. Refrigerate until ready to serve.

■ Raspberry and Opal Basil Vinegar

Red currants or black raspberries also work in this recipe, although black raspberries darken the color. Made with red raspberries, this vinegar is a deep garnet color and is both fruity and herby—an excellent choice for dressings and marinades. If your fruit is tart, or you prefer a touch of sweetness, add sugar to reduce acidity.

MAKES ABOUT 1 QUART (1 LITER)

1 pint (475 ml) ripe red raspberries
4 or 5 large sprigs 'Dark Opal' basil about 6 inches (15 cm) long
About 3 cups (710 ml) white wine or rice wine vinegar
About 1 tablespoon (15 ml) sugar, optional

Rinse and pick over the berries. Rinse the basil and spin or pat dry. Put the basil sprigs in a clean 1-quart (1-l) canning jar. The basil should fill the jar about halfway. Add the raspberries to the jar.

Heat the vinegar to barely simmering in a nonreactive pan. If using the sugar, stir it into the vinegar to dissolve. Pour the vinegar into the canning jar, filling it to 1/2 inch (1 cm) from the top. If you need to add vinegar, just pour in a little extra. Place a piece of plastic wrap over the top of the jar. Seal the jar and let it stand in a sunny window for about 4 weeks. Taste the vinegar after 2 or 3 weeks; if it tastes good to you, bottle it. The longer the fruit and herb are infused, the stronger the taste.

For bottling, pour the vinegar through a strainer lined with a paper towel or coffee filter. Use clean, pretty bottles, and add a fresh sprig of 'Dark Opal' basil. You can also keep the vinegar in the canning jar, removing the basil sprigs and leaving the berries at the bottom for color. Store the vinegar away from light, in a cool, dark place, and use within one year.

■ 'Lemon' Basil and White Wine Jelly

Use a white wine that is well-rounded, crisp and a bit dry, with some fruit. If you prefer not to use wine, substitute white grape juice. The white wine is delicate and acidic, the grape juice sweet, so the flavor will be different. You can use all 'Lemon' basil leaves, or a combination of two-thirds 'Lemon' basil and one-third sweet green basil for a little more basil flavor.

FILLS ABOUT 6 HALF-PINT (240-ML) CANNING JARS

3 cups (710 ml) white wine
1 cup (240 ml) water
2 cups (475 ml) packed basil; 'Lemon' basil and/or sweet green basil
1 package (1¾ ounces [50 g]) powdered fruit pectin

5 cups (1200 ml) sugar
About 6 small sprigs 'Lemon' basil

In a heavy-bottomed nonreactive pot, bring the wine, water, and basil to a boil. Reduce heat and simmer for 5 minutes. Remove from heat, cover, and let stand for at least 1 hour.

Remove the basil from the liquid, squeezing the leaves in order to remove excess liquid. Add the pectin to the liquid in the pot, stir, and bring the mixture to a full rolling boil (one that cannot be stirred down) over high heat, stirring constantly. Add the sugar, all at once, and return the mixture to a full rolling boil. Boil for exactly 1 minute, stirring constantly.

Place a basil sprig into each half-pint (240-ml) canning jar. Jars should be sterilized and still hot. Remove the jelly mixture from the heat and ladle into the hot jars filling them to 1/8 inch (3 mm) from the top. Wipe the rims of the jars and seal them with sterilized lids and rings, according to manufacturer's directions. Carefully invert the hot jars, let them stand for 5 minutes, then turn upright. Let stand at room temperature for 24 hours; check jars for seal. Store sealed, unopened jars in a cool, dark place for up to one year. Unsealed jars should be refrigerated and used within three weeks.

■ Buttermilk Dressing with Basil and Sundried Tomatoes

This tangy dressing is quick to make and gives a tasty contrast to mixed green salads, a simple salad of hearts of romaine, or a combination of arugula and summer-ripe tomatoes. It is a great sauce for falafels or used in place of mayonnaise on almost any sandwich—cheese, grilled chicken breast, or grilled vegetables. It's not bad on a baked potato, either.

MAKES ABOUT 1½ CUPS (360 ML)

1 cup (240 ml) lowfat (1½%) buttermilk
2 tablespoons (30 ml) sour half and half, sour cream, or mayonnaise
2 teaspoons (10 ml) basil or red wine vinegar
1 large clove garlic
3 tablespoons (45 ml) chopped sundried tomatoes packed in oil
1/4 cup (60 ml) packed basil leaves
3 to 4 dashes Angostura bitters
1/2 teaspoon (2 ml) salt
1/2 teaspoon (2 ml) sugar
Freshly ground pepper

In a blender, puree the buttermilk, sour half and half, sour cream, or mayonnaise, vinegar, garlic, sundried tomatoes, basil, bitters, salt, sugar, and pepper. Taste for salt, pepper, sugar, and vinegar. The dressing actually tastes better when prepared in advance. It will keep, covered and chilled, for up to one week in the refrigerator.

■ Italian-Style Pesto

For centuries, Italians have made pesto with a mortar and pestle; the name pesto comes from the verb pestare, which means to pound or grind. Pesto prepared in this manner is by far the best. The flavors are more intense when pounded—the garlic more pungent, the nuts sweeter and more resinous, the basil richer in perfume. Many of us now use a food processor to make pesto because it's quick and easy. Directions for both methods are given below. Traditionally, pesto is served with a flat-type noodle such as trenette, fettuccine, or linguine.

I prefer Parmigiano Reggiano for making pesto, but a less-aged Italian Parmesan such as Grana Padana may also be used. In Italy, a sheep's cheese called pecorino is often used. Depending on the time of year and the type of basil and garlic available, flavors will vary in strength, so you may have to add more of one or the other. If the pesto tastes sharp, add more Parmesan; if it is too thick, thin it with a little olive oil.

A little pesto makes a good sauce for grilled or roasted fish and vegetables, especially salmon, potatoes, eggplant, tomatoes, and squash; it's a tasty garnish for vegetable soups such as minestrone. A delicious dip for fresh vegetable crudités can be made by mixing equal parts of pesto and sour cream. Though not so wonderful as just-made, leftover pesto is still good after three or four days if kept tightly covered in the refrigerator. The top layer will darken some; just stir it in.

MAKES ABOUT 1½ CUPS (360 ML); ENOUGH TO DRESS 1 POUND (450 G) OF DRY PASTA OR ABOUT 1½ POUNDS (675 G) FRESH PASTA

5 cloves garlic, peeled and sliced
1/4 cup (60 ml) pine nuts
4 cups (950 ml) 'Genoa Green' basil leaves
Salt
1/2 cup (120 ml) freshly grated parmesan cheese
About 3/4 cup (180 ml) extra-virgin olive oil
1 pound (450 g) dry pasta or 1½ pounds (675 g) fresh pasta

Combine the garlic and pine nuts in a large mortar and crush them with the pestle into a smooth paste.

Add the basil to the mortar, a handful at a time.

Crush the leaves against the sides with the pestle.

The mixture will be a coarse, thick paste until the oil is added. Add a few pinches of salt to the mixture.

Stir in the cheeses. Drizzle the olive oil, a bit at a time, as you work it in with the pestle.

Once most of the oil is added, taste for seasoning and adjust with a little more oil, cheese, or salt.

If you are using a food processor, combine the garlic, pine nuts, basil, a few pinches salt, and a few tablespoons (about 45 ml) oil. Process until mixed.

Add the cheese and most of the remaining oil and process until smooth and homogenous.

Taste for seasoning, and add the rest of the oil, and a little more cheese or salt, if desired.

The pesto should become very smooth and there should not be any big pieces.

Cook the pasta until it is al dente. Toss the pasta with the pesto using a few tablespoons of the hot pasta water to thin the pesto so that it coats the pasta evenly. Add a few more tablespoons of pasta water if necessary. Serve immediately.

Peaches with 'Lemon' Basil Cream

Desserts and Beverages

'Lemon' or 'Anise' Basil Biscotti

Peaches with 'Lemon' Basil Cream

Citrus Sorbet with Opal Basil

Basil Infusions

Iced Tea with 'Cinnamon' Basil

Basil Bloody Mary

Lemonade with 'Lemon' Basil

■ 'Lemon' or 'Anise' Basil Biscotti

These crunchy, rusk-type cookies are fashioned after the Tuscan Biscotti di Prato but have an unusual added ingredient—basil. Going with the traditional anise flavor, I first made these with 'Anise' and 'Licorice' basil, and a few anise seeds. Inspired by the sweet, strong flavor of 'Lemon' basil, I tried it in the recipe. Both versions are very tasty, and they are virtually fat-free.

Whichever basil you choose, you will find a pleasant lingering aftertaste when you've indulged in a biscotti or two. As Joe Coca pointed out while photographing and sampling recipes for this book, the basil flavor is much more intense, and its bouquet comes through, when the biscotti are dunked in a cup of hot coffee. (Ditto with wine.)

MAKES ABOUT 4 DOZEN

About 3¹/₂ cups (830 g) unbleached flour
1/2 teaspoon (2 ml) baking powder
1/4 teaspoon (1 ml) baking soda
Large pinch salt
1¹/₂ cups (360 ml) sugar
3 extra-large eggs
1/2 teaspoon (2 ml) pure vanilla extract
About 1 tablespoon (15 ml) lemon zest or 1 teaspoon (5 ml) anise seed, bruised
Generous 1/2 cup (120 ml) chopped 'Lemon', 'Anise' and/or 'Licorice' basil leaves
2/3 cup (160 ml) sliced almonds, toasted and ground

Preheat oven to 375°F (190°C). Butter and flour two baking sheets.

In a mixing bowl, combine 3 cups (710 ml) of the flour, baking powder, baking soda, salt, and sugar, and stir to mix. Make a well and add the eggs; beat them with a fork in the well. Add the vanilla, 'Lemon' basil and zest, or 'Anise' basil and anise seed, and stir with a fork; begin mixing in the flour mixture. When most of the flour is mixed in, add the ground almonds and blend well.

Using the remaining 1/2 cup (120 ml) of flour, flour a flat surface and your hands and turn the dough out onto the floured surface. Knead the dough together; it will be sticky. As you knead, work in the remaining flour. The dough will still be slightly sticky, so use a little more flour if you must, and divide the dough into two pieces. Roll them into two cylinders about 2 to 2¹/₂ inches (5 to 6 cm) wide. Place the two cylinders on the prepared baking sheet. Bake in a preheated oven for 25 minutes.

Remove the baking sheet from the oven and reduce oven to 300°F (150°C). Slice the rolls diagonally into slices 1/2 to 3/4 inch (1 to 2 cm) thick. Arrange on two baking sheets and bake for 15 minutes. Turn the biscotti and bake for 15 minutes more.

Cool the biscotti on baking racks. Pack them into tins with tight-fitting lids. They are better the second day after baking, and keep well for a few weeks.

∎   Peaches with 'Lemon' Basil Cream

The fragrance and flavor of 'Lemon' basil combined with summer-ripe peaches is a match made in heaven. The custard cream sauce can be made well in advance. Wait to prepare the fruit so it doesn't turn dark.

SERVES 6 TO 8

6 to 8 very ripe peaches, peeled and sliced
1 tablespoon (15 ml) lemon juice
6 to 7 tablespoons (90 to 105 ml) sugar
1/3 cup (80 ml) 'Lemon' basil leaves, packed
1/2 cup (120 ml) whipping cream
1/2 cup (120 ml) milk
Pinch salt
Large handful 'Lemon' basil sprigs; about 8 or 10 sprigs 2 to 3 inches (5 to 8 cm) long
2 extra-large egg yolks
1/2 cup (120 ml) whipping cream, stiffly whipped
'Lemon' basil leaves for garnish

Toss the peaches in a bowl with the lemon juice, 1 to 2 tablespoons (15 to 30 ml) sugar, and basil leaves. If the fruit is tart, use the larger amount of sugar; if it is sweet, use less.

In a double boiler over very hot water, combine the cream, milk, remaining 5 tablespoons (75 ml) sugar, salt, and basil sprigs. Cook over simmering water for 10 minutes, stirring occasionally.

Beat the yolks in a small bowl. Pour about 1/2 cup (120 ml) of the basil cream mixture over the yolks and whisk well. Return the cream and yolk mixture to the double boiler and mix well. Cook over just-simmering water for 10 minutes, stirring, until the mixture thickens. Remove from heat and strain the custard cream through a sieve into a stainless steel bowl. Discard the basil.

Let the custard cream cool to room temperature with a piece of wax paper placed across the bowl, then chill. Or to cool quickly, place the bowl of custard cream in a larger bowl filled with ice, and stir occasionally until cooled, then chill. The cream will thicken a bit as it cools.

Remove the basil cream from the refrigerator about 10 or 15 minutes before serving. Fold the freshly whipped cream into the basil cream. Fill small dessert bowls with peaches and spoon basil cream over each serving. Garnish each dessert with a 'Lemon' basil leaf and serve immediately.

■ Citrus Sorbet with Opal Basil

Refreshing on a hot summer day, citrus sorbet is an eye-opener in the dead of winter. I dry 'Dark Opal' basil to use for just this recipe, especially since my friend Carolyn ships me a box of Lisbon lemons from the tree in her backyard in California every January. I can't begin to tell you how wonderfully aromatic, sweet, tart, and fruity these bright yellow orbs are! Suffice it to say, I salivate all the way to the post office and back. If you don't have exotic Lisbons or Meyers, regular lemons, plus ruby-red grapefruit, will do the trick. Before it is frozen, the prepared liquid is a bright rosy pink with yellow curls of zest, and when it is ready it is a fluffy, slushy medium-pink. First taste is a surprising burst of flavor, followed by tart and sweet sensations, with a blush of lingering perfume.

MAKES 1 QUART (1 LITER)

3 cups (710 ml) water
1/2 cup (120 ml) packed fresh 'Dark Opal' basil leaves or 3 tablespoons (45 ml)
  dried 'Dark Opal' basil leaves
1 cup (240 ml) sugar
2 large lemons
1 small red or pink grapefruit
Zest of 1 or 2 lemons; generous tablespoon (15 ml)

Bring 2 cups (475 ml) water and the basil leaves to a boil in a nonreactive saucepan. Boil 1 minute and add the sugar. Reduce heat and simmer over low heat for about 4 minutes, until the sugar is dissolved and the liquid is turning purple. Remove from heat and let cool to room temperature.

Meanwhile, remove the zest from the lemon. Squeeze the lemons and strain the juice, pressing on the pulp to extract as much as possible. Squeeze the grapefruit and repeat the straining process. Stir the zest and juices together; the liquid should measure 1¼ cups (300 ml).

Strain the basil and sugar syrup to remove the basil, then add the remaining cup of water. Combine the basil syrup with the fruit juice. If the mixture is chilled first, it will freeze faster.

Freeze the mixture according to the manufacturer's instructions for your ice cream maker. When it's ready, serve the sorbet in sherbet glasses or pretty bowls. If you place the sorbet in the freezer and it becomes hard, allow it to stand at room temperature for 10 or 15 minutes before scooping and serving.

■ Basil Infusions

Herb farmer and friend Don Haynie has written a little book, The Essence of Herbs, (Raphine, VA: Buffalo Springs Herb Farm, 1994) in which he discusses herbal infusions, decoctions, and tisanes. Don inspired me to go further than mint and lemon balm and I became quite taken with infusing basil. (An infusion is the flavor that is extracted from herb leaves by steeping them in hot water, as for tea, or other liquid.) The infusions can be drunk hot, they can be chilled and served like iced tea, or mixed with other drinks; or they can be poured into ice cube trays and frozen. The ice cubes then can be used to flavor all sorts of beverages. Just be sure to label your freezer bags of ice cubes because, once frozen, they all look the same.

This recipe presents the way to make an infusion using different basils, a few recipes that call for infusions follow. You will want to experiment and come up with your own uses for infusions.

MAKES ABOUT 1 QUART (1 L) OF INFUSION; FILLS 2 OR 3 ICE CUBE TRAYS

1 quart (1 l) water
Generous 2 cups (475 ml) packed fresh basil leaves; flowers can also be used

Bring the water to a boil in a nonreactive saucepan. Add the herb leaves and cover. Let steep for about 30 minutes, or until the infusion has cooled to room temperature.

Strain the herbs and pour the infusion into a glass jar or pitcher and refrigerate. You may also pour the infusion into ice-cube trays and freeze until hard. Once frozen, pop the cubes into zip-close freezer bags.

■ Iced Tea with 'Cinnamon' Basil

This is a refreshing change from iced tea with mint. Most people like their tea sweetened; if you don't, omit the sugar. Add the smaller amount for a touch of sweetness, add more for a sweet taste. Garnish glasses with a slice of orange and a sprig of 'Cinnamon' basil.

MAKES 6 TO 8 SERVINGS

2 quarts (2 l) water
3 tablespoons (45 ml) black tea or 4 teabags
About 3 cups (710 ml) 'Cinnamon' basil
1/4 to 1/3 cup (60 to 80 ml) sugar
1 orange, halved and thinly sliced
Sprigs of 'Cinnamon' basil for garnish

Bring the water to a boil in a nonreactive saucepan and remove it from the heat. Make an infusion with the water, black tea, and 'Cinnamon' basil. Stir in the sugar, if desired.

Let the infusion cool to room temperature and strain it into a glass jar or pitcher. Add the orange slices and refrigerate until cold. Serve over plain or 'Cinnamon' basil ice cubes.

■ Basil Bloody Mary

The use of fresh basil ice cubes elevates a Bloody Mary to new heights. Also use basil ice cubes in tomato, V-8, or carrot juice, or put one in your next bowl of gazpacho. Ice cubes for these liquids should be made from 'Genoa Green' or a sweet-green-basil infusions.

MAKES ABOUT 6 SERVINGS

1 quart (1 l) tomato juice or V-8 juice
1 cup (240 ml) vodka
About 1 tablespoon (15 ml) lime juice
Few dashes Angostura bitters
Few dashes Tabasco, optional
Small handful basil leaves
Basil ice cubes
6 stalks celery, washed and trimmed
Sprigs of Genoa Green basil for garnish

To make the bloody Mary mixture, combine in a pitcher the tomato or V-8 juice, vodka, lime juice, bitters, and the Tabasco if desired. Add the basil leaves and bruise against the side of the pitcher with the back of a wooden spoon. Refrigerate until chilled.

Place basil ice cubes in glasses and pour the drink mixture over them. Garnish each glass with a sprig of basil and a celery stalk for stirring or crunching.

■ Lemonade with 'Lemon' Basil

Make a simple glass of lemonade intriguing by adding 'Lemon' basil ice cubes. These ice cubes are also good in limeade, pineapple juice, iced tea, even sparkling water. Make an infusion using 'Lemon' basil and freeze into ice cubes.

MAKES 6 TO 8 SERVINGS

6 lemons
2 quarts (2 l) water

1 cup (240 ml) sugar
1 lemon, thinly sliced with seeds removed
Lemon-basil ice cubes
Sprigs of 'Lemon' basil for garnish

To make the lemonade, squeeze the juice from the lemons. Bring the water to a boil and stir in the sugar to dissolve. Add the lemon juice, stir well, and add the lemon slices. Let cool to room temperature.

Refrigerate the lemonade until ready to serve. Fill your glasses with the 'Lemon' basil ice cubes and pour the lemonade over the cubes. Add a splash of sparkling water, if desired. Garnish the glasses with 'Lemon' basil sprigs and serve.

Sources of Seeds and Supplies

Many companies offer basil seeds and plants, and seed starting supplies. Our list is not intended to be comprehensive; it mentions companies from which we obtained seeds and a few others worth noting.

Seeds and plants

Abundant Life Seed Foundation
P.O. Box 772 / 930 Lawrence St.
Port Townsend, WA 98368
(360) 385-5660. Catalog, $2.

Companion Plants
7247 N. Coolville Ridge Road
Athens, OH 45701
(614) 592-4643. Catalog, $3.

The Cooks Garden
P.O. Box 535
Londonderry, VT 05148
(802) 824-3400. Catalog, free.

Johnny's Selected Seeds
Foss Hill Rd.
Albion, ME 04910
(207) 437-4301. Catalog, free.

Native Seeds Search
2509 N. Campbell Ave. #325
Tucson, AZ 85719
(520) 327-9123. Catalog, $1.

Nichols Garden Nursery
1190 N. Pacific Highway
Albany, OR 97321
(503) 928-9280. Catalog, free.

Park Seed Company
Cokesbury Rd.
Greenwood, SC 29647
(800) 845-3366. Catalog, free.

Redwood City Seed Co.
P.O. Box 361
Redwood City, CA 94064
(415) 325-7333. Catalog, $1.

Richters
357 Highway 47
Goodwood, Ontario L0C 1A0, Canada
(905) 640-6677. Catalog, free.

Sandy Mush Herb Nursery
316 Surrett Cove Rd.
Leicester, NC 28748
(704) 683-2014. Catalog, $4.

Shepherd's Garden Seeds
30 Irene Street
Torrington, CT 06790
(860) 482-3638. Catalog, free

The Thyme Garden Herb Seed Co.
20546 Alsea Highway
Alsea, OR 97324
(541) 487-8671. Catalog, $2.

W. Atlee Burpee & Co.
Warminster, PA 18974
(215) 674-1793. Catalog, free.

Well-Sweep Herb Farm
205 Mt. Bethel Rd.
Port Murray, NJ 07865
(908) 852-5390. Catalog, $2.

Supplies

Gardener's Supply Company
128 Intervale Rd.
Burlington, VT 05401
(800) 444-6417. Catalog, free.

A. M. Leonard, Inc.
P.O. Box 816
Piqua, OH 45356
(800) 543-8955. Catalog, free.

Bibliography

Boccaccio, Giovanni. *The Decameron*. Mark Musa and Peter Bondanella, translators. New York: W.W. Norton & Co., 1977.

Bugialli, Giuliano. *The Fine Art of Italian Cooking*. New York: Quadrangle/The New York Times Book Co., 1977.

Bunt, A.C. *Modern Potting Composts*. University Park, Pennsylvania: Pennsylvania State University Press, 1987.

Child, Julia. *The Way to Cook*. New York: Alfred A. Knopf, 1989.

DeBaggio, Thomas. *Growing Herbs from Seed, Cutting, and Root*. Loveland, Colorado: Interweave Press, 1994.

della Croce, Julia. *Pasta Classica*. San Francisco: Chronicle Books, 1987.

Dille, Carolyn, and Belsinger, Susan. *Herbs in the Kitchen*. Loveland, Colorado: Interweave Press, 1992.

Edwards, John. *The Roman Cookery of Apicius*. Port Roberts, Washington: Hartly and Marks, Inc., 1984.

Foster, Gertrude., and Louden, Rosemary. *Park's Success with Herbs*. South Carolina: George W. Park Seed Co., 1980.

Gerard, John. *The Herbal or General History of Plants*. 1633 edition revised and enlarged by Thomas Johnson. New York: Dover Publications, Inc. 1975.

Grieve, Maud. *Culinary Herbs and Condiments*. New York: Dover Publications, 1971.

———. *A Modern Herbal*. New York: Dover Publications, 1971.

Hartmann, Hudson and Dale. E. Kester. *Plant Propagation*, 4th edition. Englewood Cliffs, New Jersey: Prentice-Hall, Inc., 1959.

Hazan, Marcella. *The Classic Italian Cookbook*. New York: Alfred A. Knopf, 1979.

Jeffers, Robert H. *The Friends of John Gerard*. Falls Village, Connecticut: The Herb Grower Press, 1967.

Kestner, Arlene, James E. Simon, and Arthur O. Tucker, eds. *Herbs '94, Proceedings of the Ninth National Herb Growing and Marketing Conference*. Mundelein, Illinois: Herb Growers and Marketers Association, 1994.

Laurie, Alex, D.C. Kiplinger, and Kennard S. Nelson. *Commercial Flower Forcing*. New York: McGraw-Hill Book Company, 1969.

Mastalerz, John W., ed. *Bedding Plants*. University Park, Pennsylvania: Pennsylvania Flower Growers, 1976.

Mazza, Irma Goodrich. *Herbs for the Kitchen*. Boston: Little, Brown, and Company, 1975.

Newsome, J., ed. *Pliny's Natural History: A Selection from Philomon Holland's Translation*. London: Oxford University Press, 1964.

Parkinson, John. *Paradisi in Sole Paradisus Terrestris. (A Garden of Pleasant Flowers)*. Reprint. New York: Dover Publications, Inc., 1976.

Powell, Charles C., and Richard K. Lindquist. *Ball Pest & Disease Manual*. Geneva, Illinois: Ball Publishing, 1992.

Root, Waverley. *The Food of Italy*. New York: Atheneum, 1971.

Simon, James E., Arlene Kestner, and Maureen A. Buehrle, eds. *Herbs '89, Proceedings of the Fourth National Herb Growing and Marketing Conference*. Mundelein, Illinois: Herb Growers and Marketers Association, 1989.

Slavitt, David R., translator. *The Eclogues and the Georgics of Virgil*. Garden City, New York: Doubleday, 1972.

Stobart, Tom. *Herbs, Spices, and Flavorings*. New York: Overlook Press, 1982.

Taylor, Norman. *Taylor's Guide to Vegetables and Herbs*. Revised and edited by Gordon P. DeWolf, Jr. Boston: Houghton Mifflin, 1987.

Thorne, John. *Aglio, Oglio, Basilico*. Boston: The Jackdraw Press, 1981.

Woodward, M., editor. *Leaves from Gerard's Herball*. New York: Dover Publications, 1969.

Index